Susan Hawthorne is a poet, novelist, aerialist, academic, activist and publisher. She co-founded Spinifex Press with Renate Klein fifteen years ago and works as a Research Associate at Victoria University. She has been a literary entrepreneur, organising festivals and conferences, and was chair of the 6th International Feminist Book Fair. She has been a Board member of Asialink for the last four years. Susan Hawthorne is a member of the Women's Circus and the Coalition of Activist Lesbians (COAL). She is the author of four books and (co-)editor of ten anthologies. Her novel, *The Falling Woman* was a Top Twenty Title in the Listener Women's Book Festival (NZ) and selected as one of the Year's Best Books in *The Australian* (1992), *The Spinifex Quiz Book* (1993) was shortlisted for *The Australian* Awards for Excellence in Educational Publishing, and *Wild Politics* (2002) was selected as one of the Year's Best Books in *Australian Book Review*.

other books by susan hawthorne

poetry

Bird (1999)
The Language in My Tongue. In *Four New poets* (1993)

fiction

The Falling Woman (1992)

non-fiction

Wild Politics: Feminism, Globalisation and Bio/diversity (2002)
The Spinifex Quiz Book (1993)

anthologies

HorseDreams: The Meaning of Horses in Women's Lives (2004)
(co-edited with Jan Fook and Renate Klein)
Cat Tales: The Meaning of Cats in Women's Lives (2003)
(co-edited with Jan Fook and Renate Klein)
September 11, 2001: Feminist Perspectives (2002)
(co-edited with Bronwyn Winter)
CyberFeminism: Connectivity, Critique and Creativity (1999)
(co-edited with Renate Klein)
Car Maintenance, Explosives and Love and Other Contemporary Lesbian Writings (1997) (co-edited with Cathie Dunsford and Susan Sayer)
Australia for Women: Travel and Culture (1994)
(co-edited with Renate Klein)
Angels of Power and Other Reproductive Creations (1991)
(co-edited with Renate Klein)
The Exploding Frangipani: Lesbian Writing from Australia and New Zealand (1990)
(co-edited with Cathie Dunsford)
Moments of Desire: Sex and Sensuality by Australian Women Writers (1989)
(co-edited with Jenny Pausacker)
Difference: Writings by Women (1985)

the butterfly effect

susan hawthorne

SPINIFEX

Spinifex Press Pty Ltd
504 Queensberry Street
North Melbourne, Vic. 3051
Australia
women@spinifexpress.com.au
http://www.spinifexpress.com.au

First published by Spinifex Press, 2005

Cover and book design by The Modern Art Production Group
Made and printed in Australia by McPherson's Printing Group

National Library of Australia
Cataloguing-in-Publication data:

Hawthorne, Susan, 1951- .
The butterfly effect.

Bibliography.
ISBN 1 876756 56 X.

I. Title.
A821.3

contents

note to sappho vii

the butterfly effect 1

strange tractors 3
hystory 4

unstopped mouths 9

unstopped mouths 11
empurpled 19
in the prisons 27
rose garden 37
firenze 43
death 51
gumboots and goblin fruit 55
amphibious lips 63
the land 71
angel tongues 77
tragedia 83
love is an uprising 95
lavender hour 101
carnivale 107

composition 113

music for lesbian mouths 115

dialogues with death 117

almanac of the dead 119
graveside meditation 125
ambition 128
fragments 132
sacrifice 136
the dead 137

india sutra 141

prologue 143
first sutra 147
second sutra 194
third sutra 208

fragilities 211

gravity defied 213
animal house 215
greek 216
oil and water 220
day of my crucifixion 222
song to purnulurlu 225
eye of a needle 226
the name of god is O 231

bibliography 235

acknowsledgements 247

note to sappho

It's been a long time since we conversed sitting on the cliff overlooking the sea as the waves broke on the shore far below. It was not a day for leaping off cliffs, we had more important things to do. We plucked petals, she loves me, she loves me not. We watched butterflies cavorting in the updrafts. You told me the story of the cow, her path a pattern of lines and curves, curves and lines, like the words of a poem written back and forth across a parchment. On that day we had a kind of innocence.

The world is darker now. Nearly all of us have forgotten our vows. But you – you were right – you have not been forgotten, although your poems lie broken, shattered, tiny fragments. Still they discover you. Just in the last year, another poem unearthed. Our communities too, are divided by betrayals, envy, lust for power and distrust of almost everything under the sun.

The passage has been rough. We emerge when the world is safe. Indeed, perhaps our existence is a measure of happiness. For when our lives are celebrated, there exists the kind of freedom for which we have yearned. At other times we raise storms, kick up eddies of chaos on the edge of the fathers' psyches. We have been accused of flight and of depravity. We have been violated and vilified. And yet there's a chorus just beyond the limits of audibility, we know it exists, but who will praise it?

Susan Hawthorne
July 2005

the butterfly effect

strange tractors

It's an ancient method of
ploughing— more ancient even than
boustrophedon— two cattle retracing
their steps in parallel lines

No, here there's not a
straight line to be seen anywhere— chaos
in the shape of two vulval wings—
the butterfly effect

hystory

The roses are in bloom. They are red and cool
and have a smell that makes me remember
my mother cutting stems of red roses.
        Cutting red roses

climbing the legs of the tankstand.
Mother. Roses. For how many millennia have these
images coalesced? —*in my rose-wet cave,*
        writes Adrienne Rich.[1]

Millennia ago women drew signs on walls in caves.
Signs resembling the leaves of roses doubling as vulvas.
Or stones, egg-shaped with a flowerbud
        vulva engraved on one side.

What does woman want? asks the Freud who wrote
Totem and Taboo and didn't think to include mothers
in his scheme of things. He seems to have a problem
        with the mother. Is it womb envy?

Is it that he wants to be an hysteric?
Wants access to that mysterious state
that is specific to women? What he could
        do with a floating womb!

1 Rich, Adrienne. 1978. "Twenty-One Love Poems" in *The Dream of a Common Language: Poems 1974-1977.*

We stand in a place where flowers cling to walls.
They have purple petals and we kiss beneath this wall,
remembering the women, the two women whose
        names began each with a V,

who at some time kissed beneath this same wall.
Sissinghurst. Kissing. With a V like in vulva,
like the sign of the bird goddess from
        the Upper Paleolithic.

It was women who determined the shape of
human development and of religious beliefs for
some 500,000 years, says Marija Gimbutas in a lecture
        somewhere near Hollywood.[2]

A spring day, a day that thousands of years ago
might have seen the performance of a ritual to bring the
world into being once again. The kind of ritual
        that might have involved

Baubo lifting her skirts in joy to show her vulva to
the earth, to spill her blood on fields. The kind that
prevailed until they began killing the king and ploughing
        him into the fields.

2 Marija Gimbutas. 1990. Lecture, UCLA, May 5.

Men's magic didn't work. They never returned,
in spite of the stories. *The woman does not exist,*
says Lacan, who fancies himself an hysteric.
        In fact, he goes on to say,

nothing can be said of the woman. Nothing.[3]
Nothing? Why not? asks the young woman
in the front row of the lecture theatre somewhere
        in a divided city.

Because, he replies, stretching out his
words to cover the entire history of man,
—for the girl the only organ, or to be more
        precise, the only kind of

sexual organ which exists is the phallus.
Really? replies the young woman, perplexed.
—in my rose-wet cave, writes Adrienne Rich.
        The young woman

has been reading poetry before attending
this lecture. She is puzzled by the
discontinuities of experience.
        Lacan goes on,

3 Juliet, Mitchell and Jacqueline Rose (Eds.). 1982. *Feminine Sexuality: Jacques Lacan and the École Freudienne.* Macmillan, London. Texts referred to are: "Introduction - II", Jacqueline Rose; "Feminine Sexuality in Psychoanalytic Doctrine", Jacques Lacan; "A Love Letter", Jacques Lacan.

not missing a beat. His history is his
history after all. He elaborates on his history
and gives an account of how the status of the
    phallus in human

sexuality enjoins on woman a definition
in which she is simultaneously
symptom and myth. Like Foucault's
    distrust of lived

experience, Lacan does not, cannot,
hear the young woman speak. The woman
does not exist. There is no
    feminine symbolic.

She says, *But what of those 500,000 years of*
vulvas on caves and walls and stones and pot shards?
What of the ancient language of the body of women?
    What of the body of knowledge,

the body knowledge?[4] She shouts,
but no one hears her. — *in my rose-wet cave,*
writes Adrienne Rich. *A rose is a rose*
    is a rose is a rose,[5]

4 Marija Gimbutas. 1990. *The Language of the Goddess.*
5 Stein, Gertrude. 1989. *Lifting Belly,* Rebecca Mark (Ed.).

shouts Gertrude, climbing the hill.
A stone shouts as her belly lifts to the sky.
A stone is carved with the image of a
flowerbud on one side.

Gertrude runs her finger across the stone,
lightly. *Primitive fantasies,*
mutters Freud. *Vulvas on the*
walls of caves,

caves as vulvas, wet roses—
all primitive fantasies.
Only the phallus exists,
adds Lacan,

staring out the window to where
high-rise buildings dominate the horizon.
Not far away a high wall divides
an ancient city.

At the base of the wall, breaking through
the mortar, a flower grows. Its anthers exposed
to the earth just as Baubo did on a
spring day long ago.

unstopped mouths

1 *unstopped mouths*. This title was suggested by the phrase "stopped mouths" used by Page duBois in *Sappho is Burning*, p. 37. She writes, "… the ellipses [of Sappho] in the published archaic fragments, [recall] stopped mouths, messages gone astray, the utter failure of communication across a distance of centuries, provoke discomfort." The late twentieth century has seen lesbians unstop our mouths, dig for history and intercept the messages gone astray.

2 *gymnasium*. The setting of a gymnasium arose from reading Olga Broumas and T. Begley's *Sappho's Gymnasium* (1994). Broumas and Begley write in their Proem: "Gymn: nude, trained, exposed, athletic, flexible, practice./Gymnasteon: imperative: tears unbecoming." Gymnasium also means school, and in Ancient Greece it often included a sacred grove. That women used a gymnasium is not outside the realms of possibility since the Herean Games, games for sports-women, pre-dated the Olympic Games, taking place around 1000 BC and earlier.

3 *Sappho*. Saphon, Sappho, Sapho, Sappho, Sapphô, Psappha. Joan deJean uses the above list as an indication of the process of naming. In my own life I first encountered Sapho as a schoolgirl. As a lesbian in the early 1970s I noticed that Sappho was more usual, and later when I studied Ancient Greek Psappha became my word of choice. More recently in thinking through the derivations of words, I suggest that Sappho is related to the Sanskrit Saraswati (goddess of writing), and to the French word, savoir, to know. See India Sutra, this collection, p. 171. I have used Sappho throughout this poem in the interests of familiarity. See Joan deJean's *Fictions of Sappho 1546-1937* (1989), p. 1. The question of Sappho's sexuality has been in constant dispute since antiquity, but whatever the case, Sappho has had an undeniable imaginative force for lesbians in Western culture.

4 *topmost bough*. Sappho Fragment 105a. See Page duBois, pp. 31-54, *Sappho is Burning*; also see Judy Grahn's *The Highest Apple: Sappho and the Lesbian Poetic Tradition* (1985). Judy Grahn begins her book with a translation of this fragment from David A. Campbell's literal translation in his *Greek Lyric Vol. 1* (1982), p. 131. The fragment reads: "As the sweet apple reddens on the bough-top, on the top of the topmost bough; the apple gatherers have forgotten it – no, they have not forgotten it entirely, but they could not reach it."

5 *ritual*. For more information see Giti Thadani, *Sakhiyani: Lesbian Desire in Ancient and Modern India* (1986), p. 108. Among the tribals of India women become *sahiyas*, lifelong companions. They drink rice from each other's glass, share a mango and reciprocally wash one another's feet.

6 *silkworkers*. See Janice Raymond's *A Passion for Friends* (1986), pp. 113-147; also Agnes Smedley, "Silk Workers"; for a fictional treatment see Gail Tsukiyama, *Women of the Silk* (1993). The Chinese silkworkers formed "Sister Societies" and worked together in silk factories. Janice Raymond writes about them as "marriage resisters". Their relationships were committed and maintained beyond the confines of Confucian (and Communist) family life.

unstopped mouths[1]

we meet in the gymnasium not to huff and puff and sweat into wet towels this is a gymnasium[2] for women it takes into account all the needs of the body the mind the wild spirit

here lesbians read Sappho[3] in her original tongue we converse and share our memories of families of ancestors without issue we compare family trees where a single woman sits alone on a branch she is on the topmost bough[4] with the reddest apple in her hand she is about to take the first bite the final bite perhaps she will be cast off this bough not allowed to inhabit the ordinary society of people

some of us are disguised hidden in stories of two women travelling across the land enacting their dreams we are called sisters we are hidden in ancient rituals of women's friendship where we share the same mango its juices running along our fingers and together we drink a glass of rice wine we bend toward one another caressing and washing each other's feet in anticipation[5] we work in the silk factories[6] where we tend the worms their yellow thread binding us and in imitation we braid our hair we brush the long strands with our fingers we work among books in musty libraries our hair ceremonies have

7 *disguise.* M. Barnard Eldershaw – Marjorie Barnard and Flora Eldershaw – wrote a novel, *A House is Built,* that tells the story of Mary Reiby, depicted on the Australian $20 note. Rarely are these three women acknowledged as lesbians. Marjorie Barnard shared her later life with companion, Vee Murdoch. See the interview with her by Zoë Fairbairns in *Writing Lives: Conversations between Women Writers* (1988).

8 *nameless.* Most lesbians' lives remain undocumented in the sense that either their names are known to us but their sexuality remains hidden or their sexuality is known to us but their names remain hidden. There are some writers whose names I've not cited in this poem, knowing they prefer not to be out. Perhaps some day we shall all feel able to be who we are.

9 *shards of pots.* Many of Sappho's poems are known only from fragments some of which are found on broken pottery; this reflects the fragmented history of lesbians. The most recent poem by Sappho was discovered in 2004 by researchers at Cologne University Germany, wrapped around an Egyptian mummy. The poem reads, in part: "You for the fragrant – bosomed muses' lovely gifts, by zealous girls, and the clear melodius lyre; But my once tender body old age has seized; my hair's turned white instead of dark." "Sappho Lost Poem Found" (2005).

10 *tapestry.* The Bayeaux Tapestry was made by the hands of nuns, the last section of it has been lost as visitors pulled at it, tearing it from the whole. On nuns as lesbians in a contemporary context see *Lesbian Nuns: Breaking the Silence* edited by Rosemary Curb and Nancy Mannahan (1983).

11 *to see.* Lesbians are most likely to recognise lesbian history. A great deal of lesbian history is denied by heterosexual scholars wishing to maintain the status quo.

12 *climbing mountains.* Freda du Faur (1882-1925) was the first Pakeha woman to climb Mt Cook in New Zealand's South Island. The two peaks Du Faur and Cadogan are named after her and her lover, Muriel Cadogan. In spite of their achievements, they were forcibly separated by doctors using sleep treatment, and possibly electric shock treatment, and Muriel Cadogan died as a result. See Sally Irwin. 2000. *Between Heaven and Earth: The Life of Mountaineer, Freda du Faur.*

13 *scaling octaves.* Dame Joan Hammond 1912-1996, the first Australian operatic diva to sell a million records and golfing champion who lived with her partner, Lolita Marriott for 62 years.

14 *living to a hundred and six.* Monte Punshon, born Ethel Punshon in 1882 worked in the theatre, and after travelling to China, Korea and Japan in 1929, decided to learn first Mandarin then Japanese. When war broke out she used her language skills to assist Japanese interned in camps in Australia. At 105 she attended the launch of her autobiography in Kobe. She died in 1989 aged 106. Margaret Taylor's 1989 article in *Melbourne Star Observer*, p. 1 and p. 3. Her life was included in the travelling exhibition, *Forbidden Love* which toured Australia between 1996 and 1998.

simplified a single twist of hair in a bun above a bespectacled face you wouldn't know what we do with our fingers and our hair when we desire we disguise[7] our interest in other lesbian lives writing under pseudonyms about our forebears

each day we make rituals of food sucking at artichoke hearts soaked in citrus peeling avocadoes with four hands tonguing cherries and berries of all kinds

some of us have left faint tracks which we follow into the labyrinthine hollow of memory a few words a few names Sappho foremost amongst them most remain nameless[8] we search for the lives which might never have existed lives we know only from shards of pots[9] lives and poems fragmented by time we pull at the end of the tapestry[10] and the image vanishes at the touch of each human hand

in so many places we don't exist even when the exhumed remains are on show for all to see[11] we are remembered for climbing mountains[12] scaling octaves[13] and living to a hundred and six[14]

15 *jade body*. Wu Tsao 19th century, China. In *Women Poets of China*. 1982. Translated by Kenneth Rexroth and Ling Chung. The poem ends with these lines: "I want to possess you completely–/ Your jade body/ And your promised heart./ It is Spring./ Vast mists cover the Five Lakes./ My dear, let me buy a red painted boat/ And carry you away."

16 *limbs loosening*. Sappho, a variation on Mary Barnard's translation. See Mary Barnard, *Sappho: A New Translation*. (1958) poem 53. The fragment reads: "With his venom/ Irresistible/ and bittersweet/ that loosener/ of limbs, Love/ reptile-like/ strikes me down."

17 *whistle*. In former times it was unladylike for women to whistle, only "loose women" whistled.

18 *singing songs*. Alix Dobkin has written about her life as a lesbian feminist singer. See her Minstrel Blood column in *off our backs* (1999). Alix Dobkin was one of three women who produced one of the earliest out lesbian records in the 1970s, and she is still singing and performing her work. Many singers have followed in her wake including Judy Small and Robyn Archer, Jane Siberry and kd lang.

19 *ancient rose*. A reference to a painting by Jacqui Stockdale, *Portrait of a Woman Holding an Ancient Rose*, 1995.

20 *miniature from Rajasthan*. Reproduced in Giti Thadani's *Sakhiyani*, p. 53.

21 *river*. Lakmé and Mallika go down to the river to gather flowers in *Lakmé* by Délibes. This quintessential lesbian duet was sung at the First National Lesbian Festival Concert in the Sydney Opera House in 1990 to an audience of more than 2000 lesbians.

we line the shelves of our homes with poetry we speak of your jade body[15] your limbs loosening[16] and the longing which afflicts us when love ends

the silence is filled by the tremulous note of a bone flute the sound of a glass singing at the touch of a finger the whistle from the mouth of a woman who knows she can whistle up symphonies if need be[17]

the gymnasium is a place where we can remain day in day out we can sleep there some of us sleep alone restless for a lover singing songs[18] of loss with black swans some sleep dreaming of azalea touch dreaming of impossible cities of lives not yet lived we roam the world's cities from Sydney to Venice Tokyo Prague San Francisco Varanasi Suva Shanghai and Firenze where two women dream of a third holding an ancient rose[19] anywhere there are traces

some of us lie in the arms of lovers who no longer love us or entwined in love like an Indian miniature from Rajasthan[20] some of us sleep from sheer exhaustion

the mornings are bright filled with the scent of women gathering flowers by the river[21] it's our favourite season it could be the slow waking of a winter's day with muffled sounds and woodsmoke in the air or the hot north wind of

22 *human pyramids*. A reference to the Performing Older Women's Circus, a Melbourne-based circus for women over forty which had as one of its aims the fostering of lesbian visibility.

23 *orang utan*. Malay for "old person of the forest". The mother orang utan raises her young alone; at birth the young cannot climb trees, they go on to learn everything from their mothers, they do not receive socialisation from any other quarter. The mother teaches the young to climb trees, an activity frequently pursued by tomboys.

25 *not productive*. The poets/pangolins of Suniti Namjoshi's fable were not productive, and they survived. See her poem, "The Lost Species" in *Flesh and Paper*, p. 37.

25 *words*. The words that tumble from our mouths are the many unspoken words that mean lesbian, whatever our mother tongue. See Maria Lugones. 2003. *Pilgrimages/Peregrinajes*, p. 173. Italics in the original. '*If you tell me there are no lesbians in our community, do you also mean that* "jota," "tortillera," "marimacha," "pata," *are not names for our people, within* la raza?'

summer with fire in the nostrils broken by a dive into the pool

the seasons come and go without rush we withdraw from the world for a time we rest and feed our spirits our bodies are challenged by learning to work with other bodies creating human pyramids[22] imitating the orang utan[23] Lidya her mind-map her fleeting ropes and trapezes learning to create the illusion of her many hands or her body's form moving with grace through space

in this infinite sea of pleasure hearts are mended and broken we fill one another's mouths with words with ideas which might one day flourish we squander time in fruitless wishing and wanting we are not productive[24] we listen to the wind we watch the movements of sun and moon we keep our eyes on the horizon

we unstop our mouths and we sing words[25] tumble from our pens crawl from our lips leap from our throats in a great conflagration of choruses

1 *empurpled*. "Great News! We have made it into the language", writes astrophysicist, Meryl Waugh: from the 3rd (latest) edition of *The Australian Concise Oxford Dictionary* (1997): "empurple v.tr/ 1. to make purple or red 2. to make angry."

2 *purple shift*. Red shift and blue shift describe the respective move away from or towards the observer. In measuring the speed and direction of the motion of stars wavelengths are distorted: a shift to the longer red wavelength indicates movement away from the observer; a shift to the shorter blue indicates movement towards the observer. Purple shift describes the movement of an emotion into a different dimension. Neither towards nor away, the shift represents an emotional leap of faith into another realm, away from patriarchy, and certainly out of this world. What Suniti Namjoshi calls an "unfamiliar realm".

3 *the whole world turns purple*. "Morgan [E.M. Forster] says he's worked it out and spends 3 hours on food, 6 on sleep, 4 on work, 2 on love. Lytton [Strachey] says 10 on love. I say the whole day on love. I say it's seeing things through a purple shade. But you've never been in love they say." Virginia Woolf to Vita Sackville-West, 18 February, 1927. In Louise De Salvo and Mitchell A Leaska (Eds.). 1985. *The Letters of Vita Sackville-West to Virginia Woolf*. p. 204. The history of the association of purple with homosexuality is a long one and attested to by Judy Grahn's first chapter in her history of gay and lesbian metaphor, *Another Mother Tongue: Gay Words, Gay Worlds* (1984). A poem by Anonymous entitled, "A Woman's Song: To Her Indifferent Lover" written in Latin in the eleventh century includes these lines: *"Ver purpuratum exiit / ornatos suos unduit: / aspegit terram floribus, / ligna silvarum frondibus."* Gillian Spragg has translated this poem and the verse reads: "Spring, like a queen in purple comes, / puts on her gems: / with leaves and boughs / they sing their joy for hours." Although poems celebrating nature are common throughout the history of poetry, and purple is not unusual in contexts such as this, it remains interesting that it is a lesbian-authored poem which here picks up on these images. H.D. in her imagist poetry of the twentieth century was to pick up on many of these elements in her work which resonates with allusion to Classical Greek culture. In particular, her poem, "Hyacinth" alludes to the ability of this flower to withstand the cold, to be a precursor to spring, even while the icy winds prevail. See H.D. 1983. *Collected Poems: 1912-1944*, pp. 201-206. Further, the poem by Anonymous is reminiscent of some of Sappho's work. The complete original and translation can be found on the Babel Building Site, an interactive poetry site at <http://www.spinifexpress.com.au>

4 *wolves*. The Wolf Girls at Vassar were a group of girls at Vassar women's college who cavorted at night dressed in wolf skins. They were perhaps acting out Djuna Barnes' depiction of lesbian sexuality in *Nightwood* (1936). Cristina Biaggi writes of her last year in 1959: "Gail [Ellen Dunlap] got these two wolf skins from her father, so we decided to wear them – tied over the shoulder, like Hercules – everyone else was wearing Bermuda shorts – and we went out and howled. We howled in the morning and we howled at night." Two years later the story had escalated, and Lucy Cross, writing of 1961, remarks: "some friends told me about the Wolf Girl – somebody who put on a wolf skin and went howling around the Circle in the full moon. That's for me, I thought. There's room for me." See Anne Mackay (Ed.). 1993. *Wolf Girls at Vassar*, p. 17. Vassar has also been recorded in a poem by Rita Mae Brown entitled "A Song for Winds and My Vassar Women". Rita Mae Brown. 1974. *The Hand that Cradles the Rock*, p. 50.

empurpled[1]

physicists speak of red shift I say that the purple shift[2] is more important it is when a woman falls in love for the first time with another woman and the whole world turns purple[3] today I say is a purple day

in her hands the purple aubergine they kiss under a wall of purple flowers wisteria clumped like grapes ripe with liquid a single touch is enough to make it weep

the purple shift afflicts many of us at different stages of our lives there are stories of girls sent away to boarding schools there they are meant to remain pure some of these girls have turned into wolves[4] inhabiting the night baying

5 *bay to the moon*. "I want to howl at the moon / celebrate her offerings" Tomiye Ishida. "Tsuki ga Deta", in C. Allyson Lee and Makeda Silvera (Eds.). 1995. *Pearls of Passion*. Betsy Crowell, also an alumna of Vassar, writes of another group of women in 1960: "Rumor had it that they danced under the moon in bedsheets and that they were lesbians." See *Wolf Girls at Vassar*, p. 57.

6 *infinite appetites*. A reference to Baudelaire's poem "Femmes Damnées: Delphine et Hippolyte": "*Loin des peuples vivants, errantes condamnées, / A travers les deserts courez commes les loups; / Faites votre destin, âmes désordonnées, / Et fuyez l'infini que vous portez en vous!*" Charles Baudelaire. 1857/1989. *The Flowers of Evil*, p. 370.

7 *protect them*. Novelist Christine Crow cites Baudelaire's poem in her *Miss X or the Wolf Woman* (1990). The novel explores at length lesbian passion, repression, and the relationship between a headmistress and one of her star pupils.

8 *teacher's passion*. It's not unusual for girls to fall for their women teachers, those strong-minded, independent women, nor for those women teachers to have passions for one another. Dorothy Ross, Headmistress of Melbourne Girls Grammar from 1939-1955 had a long relationship with Mary Davis, Headmistress of the Junior School, and later of St Catherine's, another girls' school nearby. Miss Ross was the model for many of her students. My mother was a student at the school during her tenure and her admiration for Dorothy Ross never dimmed. See Barbara Falk, with Cecile Trioli. 2000. *D.J. Dorothy Jean Ross 1891-1982*.

9 *an army of lovers*. A reference to Sappho, a variation on this line appears in a collection of poems written by Rita Mae Brown prior to 1971. The poem, "Sappho's Reply" reads: "My voice rings down through thousands of years / to coil around your body and give you strength, / You who have wept in direct sunlight, / who have hungered for invisible chains, / Tremble to the cadence of my legacy: / An army of lovers shall not fail." Rita Mae Brown. *The Hand that Cradles the Rock*, p. 77. I remember chanting, "an army of lovers shall never be defeated" in demonstrations of the 1970s and early 1980s.

10 *the mauve peril the lesbian plague*. These terms are used by Monique Wittig in *Across the Acheron* (1987). Monique Wittig died in early 2004 leaving behind an extraordinary legacy of lesbian-centred writing. As Carolyn Gage writes in an obituary finding Wittig's work was like unearthing "a lesbian-feminist equivalent to the Bible, or the Koran, or the Bhagavad Gita." *off our backs* (2004). For critical writings on Wittig see Namascar Shaktiri (Ed.). 2005. *On Monique Wittig*.

11 *broad daylight*. Our behaviour in the 1970s was a precursor to the "kiss ins" which were staged a decade later when "Queer" emerged.

12 *badges*. The badges we wore were many and various. Some in my collection read: LESBIANS IGNITE. HOW DARE YOU PRESUME I'M HETEROSEXUAL. RADICALESBIANS. LESBIANS ARE EVERYWHERE.

13 *eggs*. An interesting subliminal message is conveyed in the use of these missiles against lesbians.

to the moon[5] with desire satisfying their infinite appetites[6] some have been corrupted by the very ones paid to protect them[7] many a girl has longed to unravel the skeins of her teacher's passion[8]

an army of lovers[9] shall never be defeated we chant as an entire generation converts we become the lavender menace the mauve peril the lesbian plague[10] my lover and I walk the inner city streets holding hands kissing in broad daylight[11] I wear a clamour of badges[12] at night in those same streets passing youths hurl eggs at us[13]

14 *pool billiards snooker*. It is a badge of honour for lesbians to be able to play these games with flair. They have long been, and still are, an important element of lesbian culture.

15 *self-defence classes*. Many lesbians have learnt self-defence, in part, to have the ability to protect themselves (not having a man about to help them!). Lesbians of my acquaintance have excelled in aikido, tae kwondo, judo, karate and ju jitsu.

16 *hunters*. Monique Wittig and Suniti Namjoshi have both depicted men as hunters in their writings. *Across the Acheron*, tells of the ritual hunt in which men pursue women in the chapter entitled "Count Zaroff's Hunt", pp. 36-39. A metaphor for aggressive sexuality, one can see the hunt in any red light district in the world. Namjoshi depicts her hunters pursuing the wolf and the virgin. Suniti Namjoshi. 1993. *St Suniti and the Dragon*, p. 86-87.

17 *streets*. Barbara Hammer in her film *Tender Fictions* (1995) says she has been attacked in the street, thrown out of a restaurant because, as she says "I am a visible lesbian".

18 *bars*. There are lots of lesbian books which look at this aspect of lesbian culture. Perhaps the most evocative story of the bar scene in the US is Lesley Feinberg's *Stone Butch Blues* (1993).

19 *underworld*. See Judy Grahn. 1984. *Another Mother Tongue*, pp. 28-33. Monique Wittig's, *Across the Acheron* is a retelling of a descent to hell, à la Virgil's descent, set in contemporary San Francisco and led by a woman named Manastabal.

20 *Ereshkigal*. See Judy Grahn. 1987. *The Queen of Swords*. An outstanding recreation of the mythic tale of a descent to the underworld. In this instance the ancient Sumerian myth of Inanna and Ereshkigal is told in the contemporary setting of the underground lesbian bar.

21 *pack*. "Ironically groups of nuns or Lesbians are often mistaken for one another today, since we often travel in female packs oblivious to male attention or needs." Rosemary Curb and Nancy Manahan (Eds.). *Lesbian Nuns: Breaking Silence*, p. xx.

22 *Hondas their Kawasakis their Harley Davidsons and their Ducatis*. The group, Dykes on Bikes, is an informal lesbian institution. In Melbourne and Sydney each year they parade as part of Midsumma or Mardi Gras, roaring their engines in mockery of masculinity, but also as a way of saying, these toys are not just for the boys. With social skills such as having a good eye for pool, or excelling at martial arts, lesbians thumb their noses at prescriptive femininity. Monique Wittig in her allegorical *Across the Acheron* describes this aspect of lesbian culture: "As I began to shout ... a string of dikes appeared, naked on their motor cycles, their skin gleaming black or golden, and one after the other they rode over the hill." p. 18.

23 *sing at the top of their lungs*. They are of course singing, "Leader of the Pack". As a young lesbian this song was one of the few pop tunes to speak to me directly in a way that captured my experience.

24 *diesel-driven road-trains*. Diesel dykes can be found behind the wheel of many means of locomotion. Road-trains ply Australia's outback, sometimes with as many as three articulated sections.

25 *relationships*. "Yeah cars are easier to deal with than people. You buy a car and you have it. You don't need to seduce it or talk to it or admit anything." Donna Jackson. 1997. "Car Maintenance, Explosives and Love", p. 68.

we play pool billiards and snooker[14] in seedy bars until the early hours of the morning the self-defence classes[15] we have taken give us the confidence to kick at the stalkers and hunters[16] who roam the streets[17] and gaming houses

we congregate in bars[18] inhabiting an underworld[19] dressed to kill to woo to impress but Ereshkigal[20] is no longer alone not only has her sister Inanna joined the pack[21] but many have turned feral as in earlier ages we became nuns

in packs we roar through the streets on our Hondas our Kawasakis our Harley Davidsons and our Ducatis[22] where there's smoke there's fire and dykes on bikes make plenty of both to sing at the top of our lungs[23] to dance as close as we can

cars too thrill us an antique Morris Minor an FJ Holden or an urban-crawling Chevrolet some of us have diesel-driven road-trains[24] or pick-up trucks we name our cars we develop relationships[25] with them and the women who ride with us

26 *solo around the world*. Amelia Earheart is a pervasive lesbian hero. Photographs of her in lesbian publications usually depict her in her flying gear, standing in front of the aircraft.

27 *pack of women*. Robyn Archer's musical theatre takes an ironic view of a pack of women playing cards in a smoke-filled bar. The success of the show is indicated by the range of forms it has taken: it was performed in theatres, and turned into a TV program, and later published as a book. Robyn Archer. 1986. *Pack of Women*.

28 *lesbian*. An alternative list to this is given by Marchessault. "The angel makers, witches, hysterical women, the bad fucks, old cows, bitches in heat, wild cats, old mares, birds of ill omen, non-virgins, whores, lesbians, unnatural mothers, loose women, crazy ladies, chattering magpies, cock teasers, the depressed and sluts, like those two there, have already been burnt, and they will be hanged on top of that." Jovette Marchessault. 1985. *Lesbian Triptych*, p. 87. Faiseuse d'ange [angel makers] is a Quebec expression denoting women who perform illegal abortions. The confounding of lesbians with other independent women is a common slippage in masculine discourses of abuse, and lesbian authors recite these words as a means of exorcism. See also: "There are rivers in my hands, my fingers are webbed like a delta. My arms have become wings and I am a witch soaring on magic flying ointment. Others fly near me – Hecate, Circe, Medea, Sappho – and their words burn into my flesh. I am tattooed with the words that killed them: witch wicce witga vitki wit wisdom wise woman / incantatrix lamia lesbian saga maga malefica / sortilega strix venefica herberia / anispex auguris divinator janutica / ligator mascara phitonissa stregula". Susan Hawthorne. 1992. *The Falling Woman*, p. 150.

harpies sirens birds of prey lesbians are accused of carrion deeds birdlike some fly donning a leather pilot's cap a windproof jacket thick with lambskin flying breeches and boots a licence to carry others or fly solo around the world[26]

in spite of sanctions we have always lived to the full wildly outrageously we've been feared for our independence our direct speech because we ride horseback but not side-saddle

four make a table for cards poker gin rummy 500 euchre whist solo and bridge they play in smoke-filled rooms each seeking her own queen a pack of women[27] each with her own magic pack of cards

the names we are called are as varied as our ways of living lesbian[28] sapphist dyke tommy girl witch companion lover shrew amazon wolf girl virago man-hater redstocking bluestocking friend partner

1 *criminals*. To be a lesbian in some places is to be a criminal. In Tasmania during the late 80s and early 90s lesbians could be arrested for their sexual practice. Among those sent to the gas chambers by Nazis were a significant number of lesbians. Upon searching for the key words "Islam lesbian" on the internet, the message came up "no match". This is rather like China's denial of lesbian existence in the People's Republic. There are countries where being a lesbian carries an immediate jail sentence, places like Algeria, Burkina Faso, Ethiopia, Morocco, Tunisia, the Bahamas, Trinidad and Tobago, Antigua and Barbuda, Barbados, Oman and Romania. Persecution, however, extends to countries where theoretically to be a lesbian is not an infringement of the law, but in reality it remains so. This is the case in Colombia, Nicaragua, Sri Lanka, Brazil. Death is the penalty in Afghanistan, Bahrain, Iran, Kuwait, Mauritania, Qatar, Saudi Arabia, Chechen Republic, Sudan, Taiwan and Yemen. Amnesty International. 1997. *Breaking the Silence: Human rights violations based on sexual orientation*, pp. 77-90. As Lillian Faderman argues, the real crime of lesbians is claiming men's freedoms for themselves. For this, lesbians have been executed as was Catharine Margaretha Linck, an eighteenth-century German who disguised herself as a man, fought as a soldier, and was executed in 1721. Lillian Faderman. 1981. *Surpassing the Love of Men*. pp. 51-2. Also see Susan Hawthorne. 2004a. "Research and Silence."

2 *tattoos*. Since the 1990s tattoos have become fashion accessories even in the mainstream. A significant number of working-class lesbians sported tattoos many years earlier. This might indicate that lesbians are part of the fashion avant garde!

3 *safer that way*. Silence has often been used as a defence by lesbians. To speak out was to risk exposure, arrest, sometimes death.

4 *Botany Bay*. Numerous women were transported to Botany Bay by the British government, many for petty crimes. Among them are bound to have been some lesbians, women with a tendency to independence and rebellion, refractory girls, as the women convicts were called. For further information on women convicts see Portia Robinson. 1988. *The Women of Botany Bay: A Reinterpretation of the Role of Women in the Origins of Australian Society*. For a poetic treatment of the same material see Jordie Albiston's *Botany Bay Document* (1996).

5 *instead*. An alternative story is told in Sara Hardy's play, "Queer Fruit". The horse is stolen to help her lover and friend who'd been caught pocketing an egg and taken to London after being convicted. The first woman is transported to Norfolk Island where she dies at the hands of the brutal jailers, the second is transported to New South Wales where she begins a new life, does not marry, and runs her own farm, as do Anne Drysdale and Caroline Newcomb on the outskirts of Geelong, near Melbourne. They are known locally as the "Lady Squatters".

in the prisons

we are known as criminals[1] not by family not by inheritance but by association some of us are hardened some were out of luck many are innocent

our differences are hidden in our faces our eyes the shape of our mouths the lines that mark us we bear our marks proudly scars tattoos[2] faces creased with pain the words we speak are sparing like the Jesuits we answer only the question asked it's safer that way[3]

the crimes that define us are legal fictions change the definition and the crime ceases to exist one was pulled in for conspiracy a plot she had no part in she was crossing a border with the wrong person they arrested her for her associations they arrested her for politics not justice then they tortured her a fortnight of fear and deprivation they taunted her with words and with silence with knives and light and darkness she's still here and the charge is not clear

another is here for stealing a horse they're about to deport her to Botany Bay[4] along with a shipload of others whose main crime is poverty the horse was to help her sister get to a safe house so she could give birth she never got there she died instead[5]

6 *for loving other women*. Lesbians have a long association with prisons. Lesbians have been put under house arrest by husbands, fathers, brothers to prevent amorous liaisons. By contrast, jails have provided opportunities for relationships. The connection lesbians feel for women imprisoned is best represented by the popular Australian television drama of the late 1970s, *Prisoner*. *Prisoner* was a source of much gossip in the lesbian community, much of it focused on the character Frankie, who was one of the earliest "out" representations of lesbians on Australian TV.

7 *muslims christians jews buddhists hindus and mormons*. Lesbians are to be found in all communities, whatever denials there might be. See the following books for information on the intersection between lesbian existence and a range of different religions. Chava Frankfort-Nachmias and Erella Shadmi (Ed.). 2005. *Sappho in the Holy Land: Lesbian Existence and Dilemmas in Contemporary Israel*. Irshad Manji. 2003. *The Trouble with Islam: A Muslim's Call for Reform of Her Faith*; Bernadette J. Brooten. 1996. *Love Between Women: Early Christian Responses to Female Homoeroticism*; Rosemary Curb and Nancy Manahan (Eds.). 1985. *Lesbian Nuns*; Elana Dykewomon. 2003. *Beyond the Pale*; Evelyn Torton Beck (Ed.). 1982. *Nice Jewish Girls: A Lesbian Anthology*; Amiel Courtin-Wilson. 2000. *Chasing Buddha* (film); Giti Thadani. 1996. *Sakhiyani*; Suniti Namjoshi. 2000. *Goja: An Autobiographical Myth*;. Deepa Mehta. 1996. *Fire* (film). Paula Gunn Allen. 1986. *The Sacred Hoop*. Sue-Ann Post. 2005. *The Confessions of an Unrepentant Lesbian Ex-Mormon*. There are many other sources on cultures ancient, modern and Indigenous. Some are referred to in this poem.

8 *human rights advocates*. "No one is proud of dykes not families not neighbours not friends not workmates not bosses not teachers not mentors not universities not literature societies not any nation not any ruler not any benefactor not any priest not any healer not any advocate. Only other dykes are proud of dykes. People say live and let live but why should we?" Gillian Hanscombe. 1992. *Sybil: The Glide of Her Tongue*, p. 7.

9 *terrified*. Terror and fear of punishment, violence, exile and imprisonment is the lot of many lesbians. Tsitsi Tiripano (a pseudonym meaning *mercy* Tsitsi, *we're here* Tiripano) became a member of GALZ, Gays and Lesbians of Zimbabwe, a country in which lesbians are not recognised as existing but President Mugabe is vocally homophobic and in 1996 said that he believed "gays and lesbians were 'lower than pigs and perverts' and therefore 'have no rights'." Jenn Smith. 2000. *off our backs*, Vol. 30, No. 4, pp. 1 and 6-7; Liz Welch. 2000. *Ms Magazine*, June/July. pp 12- 15. There are similar instances of forced marriage, rape, imprisonment and torture in Namibia, Uganda and Zambia. South Africa remains the only country in the world to protect the constitutional rights of lesbians and gay men.

10 *Ophelia*. See "Ophelia" in Sandy Jeffs. 2000. *Poems from the Madhouse*. pp. 34-35. The other prison to which lesbians have been confined is the mental asylum.

11 *St Joan*. Joan of Arc is a heroine for many lesbians. She is reminiscent of the ancient amazons, the woman warrior on horseback, fighting for a just cause. Robin Morgan writes: "It seems, you see, there was a woman / named Haivette, / with whom Joan lived, loved, slept, / and fought in battle,/ Robin Morgan. ND. *Monster*. p. 71. This pirate edition was published by a group of lesbians in Melbourne.

12 *Chloe and Olivia*. These women appear in Virginia Woolf's *A Room of One's Own* (1929). Perhaps they have been imprisoned because they were so up front about their sexuality.

it's still happening just two days ago a young one was pulled in for theft she was homeless thrown out by her relatives for being a lesbian it was food she'd taken

many are here for loving women[6] they come from all times and places there are muslims christians jews buddhists hindus and mormons[7] and some who name no god at all no one has fought for them not even human rights advocates[8] we must fight for ourselves and when we do we are arrested terrified[9] tortured it's not about guilt simply the need for a conviction

there is a woman who sits in the corner all day she speaks only to herself or to another unseen by us she calls out to Mary Mother of God she cries out to Ophelia[10] she sings snatches of opera Lakmé St Joan[11] she calls herself mad each day her name is different it is Alla Jenny Lucy Muriel Virginia and her friends Chloe and Olivia[12]

13 *we go mad together*. Robin Morgan's poem "Monster" concludes her collection of the same name. She writes: "May my hives bloom bravely until my flesh is aflame / and burns through the cobwebs. / May we go mad together my sisters. / May our labor agony in bringing forth this revolution / be the death of all pain. // May we comprehend that we cannot be stopped. // May I learn how to survive until my part is finished. / May I realize that I /am a / monster. I am // a / monster. / I am a monster.// And I am proud." Robin Morgan. *Monster*, pp. 85-86.

14 *evil eye*. The evil eye is associated with powerful women, the archetypal figure in western mythology is Medusa, but there are many others elsewhere. For more on the archeological record of the Eye Goddess, see Marija Gimbutas, 1989. *The Language of the Goddess*, pp. 50-61. According to Barbara Walker, women who met men with a direct glance were considered to have the evil eye. "'proper' women keep their glance lowered in the presence of men." Barbara Walker. 1983. *The Woman's Encyclopedia of Myths and Secrets*, p. 295.

15 *hooliganism*. Alla Pitcherskaia, a lesbian from Russia, was charged with the crime of "hooliganism" because she continued to to work with a lesbian youth organisation. Amnesty International 2001. *Crimes of Hate*, p. 20.

16 *witchcraft*. When the European colonisers first came to the shores of Great Turtle Island (North America) the power of women in Native American communities was curbed. Paula Gunn Allen writes that lesbians were as powerful in "medicine" and that this can lead to charges of witchcraft not only from non-Indigenous American but also from Native men who may fear the spirit power of lesbians. See Paula Gunn Allen. 1986. *The Sacred Hoop*, pp. 245- 261. In the European world many lesbians and independent women were accused as heretics and burned at the stake. The catherine wheel is a cultural memory of one such method of torture and death.

17 *borderlands*. Lesbians live their lives straddling at least two cultures, what I have called the metaxu (Gr. μεταξυ) the between world. Gloria Anzaldúa refers to this as the borderlands, a place that is both physical and clearly marked but also emotional and indeterminate. As Anzaldúa writes it can also be a place of fear and hardship. "This is her home/a thin edge of/barbwire." Gloria Anzaldúa. 1987. *Borderlands/La Frontera: The New Mestiza*, pp. 3-13. Also see her poem "To live in the Borderlands means you" which continues: "are neither *hispana india negra española/ni gabacha, eres mestiza, mulata,* half-breed/caught in the crossfire between camps". Ibid, pp. 194-5. For more on the concept of metaxu (although not in a lesbian context) see my 1993 essay "Diotima Speaks through the Body" in Bat-Ami Bar On (Ed.). *Engendering Origins*.

18 *disappeared*. Among the disappeared of Argentina, Chile, Uruguay were politically active lesbians. In Chile, Consuelo Rivera-Fuentes was arrested. She survived and has written about her experience. See Consuelo Rivera-Fuentes and Lynda Birke. 2001. Talking With/In Pain: Reflections on bodies under torture. *Women's Studies International Forum*. Likewise lesbians have been among the persecuted under other regimes, among the best documented being the Nazi Regime. For one personal story see Erica Fischer. 1996. *Aimée and Jaguar*. Or, as philosopher Jeffner Allen points out: "Whenever the profiles of my memory, like the horizons of time, are erected by men, I cannot remember myself. At such moments, male domination not infrequently forces me to remember myself as essentially and 'by nature' the Other who 'is' only in relation to me. I, dismembered, disappear into nonexistence." Jeffner Allen. 1986. *Lesbian Philosophy: Explorations*, p. 13.

when the moon rises full in Scorpio we go mad together[13] some are here for invented crimes for carrying the evil eye[14] for hooliganism[15] for witchcraft[16] for healing for mysticism for whistling or dancing in the street for being in the wrong place at the wrong time for inhabiting borderlands[17]

some are here for no known crime no one knows they are here no family no friend no mother no acquaintance no stranger no lover in Argentina Uruguay Chile they simply disappeared[18] and then there are those of us prisoners who know why we are here just or otherwise

19 *best reason in the world*. Some lesbians have killed men who have abused them over many years. Among them have been husbands, brothers, fathers.

20 *it was Pauline's mother they killed*. The now famous case of Pauline Parker and Juliet Hulme which occurred in Christchurch, New Zealand in June 1954. The story can be read from a lesbian perspective in Julie Glamuzina and Alison J. Laurie's *Parker and Hulme* (1991). The film *Heavenly Creatures* (1994) deals with the material in a more populist way. In 1998 *Matricide: The Musical* took up the story of these two women in a theatrical, physical, operatic piece written by Kathleen Mary Fallon and composed by Elena Kats-Chernin for Chamber Made Opera. The set involved the audience being led into a barbed-wire prison enclosure for the performance.

21 *lesbian vampire*. The so-called lesbian vampire killers of Brisbane shot to international fame when they killed a man who had accepted a ride in their car. The media focused most on the lesbian sexuality of the women, and in particular alleged blood rites by Tracey Wiggington.

22 *patriarchy power*. Valerie Solanas was one of the first in this latest wave of feminism to express the need to kill men in order to end patriarchy. She writes, "if women don't get their asses in gear fast, we may very well all die." Valerie Solanas. 1967. *SCUM Manifesto*. p. 24. Solanas drew attention to herself by shooting Andy Warhol. Since then the most public expression of this force has been explored in films such as *A Question of Silence* (1982), *I Shot Andy Warhol* (1996) and *Love Serenade* (1996).

23 *beard*. Lesbians who have beards because they happen to have more hair grow on their faces than is socially acceptable are sometimes mistaken for young gay men. A women's liberation slogan of the 1970s ran along the lines: we love ourselves only as much as we love our sisters with hair on their faces. Bearded lesbians were frequent spectacles in the "freak shows" of the nineteenth and early twentieth centuries. In contemporary Western culture the hairless woman is the prescribed norm, but in many other cultures bearded women earn respect, as it is often a signature of age and wisdom.

my friend Daisy killed her husband it was premeditated it was provoked it was murder but she had the best reason in the world[19]

Pauline and Juliet did not have such a good reason it was youth it was terror it was love it was Pauline's mother they killed[20]

Tracy was called a lesbian vampire[21] she killed a man she did not know any man they said she had no reason at all she said no reason other than patriarchy power[22] and the belief men have that getting in a car with four women is not only safe but exciting

six-foot tall Jake is in because she has hair on her face she wears a beard[23] and they arrest her constantly because they think she's an eighteen-year old youth looking for trouble she's past forty but the skin on her cheeks is as smooth as silk

the prisons have become more crowded there are women here from places I've only ever seen named on a map from countries torn by war shredded by bombs countries where what lies underground is more important than the people who live there from lands where women are shrouded where the walls are carried by their bodies wars in which bodies are bombs

24 *white.* Eva Johnson's play, "What Do They Call Me?" explores the life of Alison, an Aboriginal lesbian who is part of Australia's stolen generation. She writes: "How do I justify being taken from my mother / being put into government institutions / being given to white mothers, who got paid / who were subsidized to raise me WHITE." Eva Johnson. 1990. "Alison". In Cathie Dunsford and Susan Hawthorne (Eds.). *The Exploding Frangipani*, p. 142. The play has subsequently been published in full in Dale Spender (Ed.). 1991. *Heroines*, and in Bruce Parr. (Ed.). 1996. *Australian Gay and Lesbian Plays*.

25 *Jermaine*. Jermaine Hicks, a character in the novel, *Push* by Sapphire. The reader can read Jermaine's life story in the appendix to the novel under the title, Harlem Butch. Sapphire. 1997. *Push*.

26 *Voudou*. See Luisah Teish. 1988. *Jumbalayah*.

27 *Afrekete*. See Catherine E. McKinley and Joyce DeLaney (Eds.). 1995. *Afrekete: An Anthology of Black Lesbian Writing*. Afrekete is a Yoruba goddess and a character from Audre Lorde's *Zami* (1982).

28 *explosives*. "Car Maintenance, Explosives and Love" by Donna Jackson is a monologue which explores the explosiveness of a relationship between a working-class and a middle-class lesbian. The play uses real explosives, handled by writer and performer, Donna Jackson. This anthology was preceded by *The Exploding Frangipani*. As Radicalesbians said in 1970: "A lesbian is the rage of all women condensed to the point of explosion." See Rosemary Silva (Ed.). *Lesbian Quotations*, p. 18.

29 *suffragists*. The anti-property strategy of the suffragists was an original approach to civil disobedience. They targeted the playgrounds of the aristocracy, including pouring acid on golf courses, thereby disrupting the pleasures of wealth.

30 *Valerie*. Valerie Solanas, author of the *SCUM Manifesto*, was very influential during the 1970s. Her small book, like the pirated edition of Robin Morgan's *Monster*, was passed from hand to hand. Perhaps its most influential idea was that members of SCUM would always subvert the system, wherever they were working. Such women would, of course, be incognito and difficult to trace. A recent edition of her book was released to coincide with the release of the movie, *I Shot Andy Warhol*. In her novel *Darkness More Visible* (2000) Finola Moorhead plays with the legacy of Valerie Solanas with a revolutionary cybercell called the Solanasites.

31 *guerilla*. Because the second wave of the women's movement coincided with the wars of liberation in the 1960s, the concept of guerilla was very current in the early 1970s. There were radical women all around the world who took up arms or who identified with far left wing "terrorist" groups. Lesbians were active in the Symbionese Liberation Army, and were probably involved in the capture of Patti Hearst. In Germany, lesbians were immediately suspect in the eyes of the state. A friend was held at gunpoint by German police who believed that she and her companions were members of the Bader Meinhof Gang. Monique Wittig taps into this zeitgeist with her novel *Les Guérillères*. Monique Wittig. 1972. *Les Guérillères*. A more recent, and more irreverent use is *The Guerrilla Girls' Bedside Companion to the History of Western Art* (1998).

32 *Glorious Age*. A period of history proposed by Monique Wittig and Sande Zeig. Roughly it equates with the beginnings of the second wave of the women's movement in the late 1960s and early 1970s. Monique Wittig and Sande Zeig. 1979. *Lesbian Peoples*.

33 *next five years*. Such stories are not unusual among lesbians in prison. A rebellious streak, added to by circumstances of poverty and bad luck, creates fertile ground for drug abuse and the resulting criminal lifestyle required to sustain it.

some live in prisons without walls but prisons all the same they have been separated stolen encased in a cocoon of white[24] walls called culture they cry for the loss of their mothers their sisters their culture

my friends Iris Elsie Sojourner Jermaine[25] are here because their skin is black in the cells they practise the ancient craft of Voudou[26] they make greetings to Afrekete[27] Oya and others they tell me only what I need to know sometimes they protect me sometimes they cannot for they are more at risk

I am here for a concatenation of reasons it started when I was just a girl shoplifting for my mother and my sisters our father long gone I skipped school was labelled a truant a troublemaker at sixteen I got my first tat a tear rolling from the corner of my left eye I was arrested more often than anyone else I knew I became an activist sat in trees lay on the road in front of bulldozers went on demonstrations got arrested again tallied up an impressive record then I got into explosives[28] like the suffragists[29] before me I began with men's property followed in the footsteps of Valerie[30] became a guerrilla[31] of the Glorious Age[32] it didn't take much to get involved in criminal activity

this time I'm here for drugs it's easy money when your luck is in mine wasn't I'm here for the next five years[33]

1 *roses and lavender*. Gertrude Jekyll recommends this in her 1902 classic, *Roses for English Gardens*. Lavender has ancient associations with lesbians. In 1970 US lesbians were wearing Lavender Menace T-shirts at protests, see Karla Jay's *Tales of the Lavender Menace* (1999). A Scottish bookshop of the 1970s and 80s was named The Lavender Menace, while a popular US lesbian band comprised of Alix Dobkin, Kay Gardner and Pat Mochetta (aka Patches Adams) called its first album, *Lavender Jane Loves Women*.

2 *violet*. Like lavender, violet has been used to signify lesbian presence. Irene Zahava in the USA has published several collections of lesbian stories under the imprint of Violet Ink.

3 *rosewater*. Rosewater, it is said, was invented by women. By one account the mother-in-law of the Persian princess Nour-Dijan noticed the scented foam which "had formed on the rivulets of rosewater that ran through the garden." In another account of the same event it was the princess herself who dipped "her handkerchief in the water as she was rowed across a small lake" She then wrung out the scented rosewater into a bottle. See John Fisher. 1986, *The Companion to Roses*, pp. 15-16.

4 *petals and hips*. Fisher writes, "The early rosaries were made up of rose petals, strung together and, later, rose hips may have been used instead. See John Fisher. 1986, *The Companion to Roses*, p. 165.

rose garden

those who have no memory struggle to find it those who have lost must invent we search our histories in unlikely places in fields along grassy verges of streams by the sea's edge in gardens

our fingers burrow seeking the unnamed the unmentionable fingers plough furrows in moist soil dig scrape tend water and watch love grow you stand in the garden wearing riding boots and jodhpurs planning the season's activities shall we plant roses or delphiniums poppies or ranunculus peony or cyclamen shall we mix roses and lavender[1] gather violets[2] at the edge of the bed at the edge of a dream or shall we go native

you dream of swathes of colour rising out of the green I crush the petals of roses inhaling the perfume together we bite into Turkish delight flavoured with rosewater[3] some bend to fill their noses with the scent of roses and Gertrude Stein chants her endless refrain others recite their cycle of prayers to the Virgin as they finger petals and hips[4]

the women of the Ladies' Auxiliary gather for afternoon tea and gossip sharing tips on how to make their gardens grow their hands are constantly busy knitting knotting

5 *Dorothy Perkins* and *Mrs Van Rossem* are the names of two roses listed in the Index of Vita Sackville-West. 1987. *The Illustrated Garden Book,* p. 190.

6 *seven sisters Danae dusky beauty assembly of beauties* (Assemblages des Beautés) *Penelope* are all names of roses listed in the Index of Vita Sackville-West's *The Illustrated Garden Book,* p. 190.

7 *give her roses.* Suniti Namjoshi, in her 1980 poem writes, "I give her the rose with unfurled petals/ she smiles / and crosses her legs. / I give her the shell with the swollen lip. / She laughs. I bite / and nuzzle her breasts. / I tell her, 'Feed me on flowers / with wide open mouths,' / and slowly, / she pulls down my head." This poem and accompanying photographs of roses and other flowers are contained in Lariane Fonseca. 1992. *If Passion Were a Flower…*

8 *ring-a-ring o' roses.* This children's rhyme is thought to have arisen in London during the Great Plague of 1665. The roses are the circular red spots, or buboes, characteristic of the plague. One form of the plague – the Pneumonic plague – is spread by sneezing.

making rosettes embroidering pillowslips damask table cloths and napkins occasionally they combine forces to make tapestries rugs or quilts

Dorothy Perkins and Mrs Van Rossem[5] tell one another stories there is a story they tell that the rosette of a nearby cathedral was built entirely by a team of women they whisper their names they were seven sisters daughters of a seventh daughter they called them the Danae they say that among them was a dusky beauty one of an assembly of beauties one called Penelope[6] they say it was she who designed the window's florets

we cast a golden rose on Sumerian jewellery and in Crete we confuse the archaeologists by restoring the damaged fresco with a six-petalled rose of course we know there are five petals five fingers but they thought we had created a fiction if it takes our fancy we still paint images of ancient roses fictions of our inventiveness

we watch our gardens grow when we fall in love we give the beloved roses[7] when she dies the roses wreathe her or are laid upon her grave we dance in circles singing ring-a-ring o' roses[8] a pocketful of posies ah-tishoo ah-tishoo we all fall down

9 *roses as white as roses are red*. Japan's most famous lesbian writer, Yoshikö Nobuya, is the author of a story, "Red Rose, White Rose". One of a series of stories in her collection *Hana Monogatari* (*Flower Stories*). "Yoshiya Nobuko (1896-1973) is the most famous and successful closeted lesbian writer in Japan." For further information on Yoshiya Nobuko, her partner Monma Chiyo and other Japanese lesbians see Marou Izumo and Clare Maree. 2000. *Love upon the Chopping Board*, pp. 78-89.

10 *blue moon*. A name of a rose listed in the Index of Vita Sackville-West's *The Illustrated Garden Book*, p. 190.

11 *dew slides across the surface*. See Lariane Fonseca. 1992. *If Passion Were a Flower...*, p. 15.

12 *wild roses*. Susan Howe in her Introduction to *The Birth-Mark: Unsettling the Wilderness in American Literary History* (1993. p. 21) writes of the antinomy of American poets Anne Hutchinson and Emily Dickinson, lamenting the lack of scholarly attention paid to these two women. The final phrase of her introduction is, "wild roses are veils before trespass". Thanks to Sue Fitchett for drawing my attention to the work of Susan Howe.

we fall upon one another kissing brushing lips against mouth against cheek against nipple against roses there and there and there

climbing roses fall in cascades from the pergola passing beneath the blooms the scent of rose oil is overwhelming the roses hang in all their glory roses as white as roses are red[9] black roses veined with red roses in hues of orange and pink yellow and mauve roses as rare as a blue moon[10]

we paint still lifes and fashion wallpapers and fabrics we photograph each bloom trying to capture the moment when dew slides across the surface of a petal[11]

we weave damask cloth stitch roses on to footstools and from time to time we cut the blooms from the bush

not for us the crown of thorns or a briar of wild roses[12] to fight our way through we cultivate the thorns as much as the flowers petals are strewn across the path into the garden entry is simple if you know the ways the trick is in how you place your fingers how you cup the bloom how you approach

we have a map we invent a terrain we find our way into and through the rose garden

1 *two women*. There are stories in many cultures about two women travelling across large tracts of land together. These tales tell of co-operation and creativity. Such tales are abundant among Indigenous peoples from northwest Australia.

2 *ancient rose*. The rose has often been equated in lesbian poetry with female genitalia. It gives new meaning to Gertrude Stein's "a rose is a rose is rose". Nossis in 325 B.C. wrote: "But one whom Kypris / Has not loved, will never know / What roses her flowers are." See Jacqui Stockdale's painting, entitled *The Memory: Portrait of a Woman Holding an Ancient Rose* (1995).

3 *flying horse*. The horse is also associated with lesbian sexuality, while the Vily of middle European legend threaten men's sexuality. Robyn Smith. "The Vily". In Susan Hawthorne, Cathie Dunsford and Susan Sayer (Eds.). 1997. *Car Maintenance, Explosives and Love and Other Contemporary Lesbian Writings*, pp, 278-280.

4 *brick*. Suniti Namjoshi, in *Building Babel*, wants to build culture on the Internet. She writes: "What I had in mind was a palace in the air and under the sea, a structure that was both real and impossible ..." (p. 34) and so, "The Black Piglet and Sister Solitude set about sorting all the things they might use. They decide that ... all bricks either could or did or even might or should, carry a message, and that therefore all bricks should be saved." Suniti Namjoshi. 1996. *Building Babel*, p. 38.

5 *ritual*. Hair rituals are practised in many cultures as a symbol of a girl's or woman's progression through the various stages of life. They are also practiced as courtship and fidelity vows between women.

6 *Firenze*. In the Biblioteca Laurenziana in Firenze you can see one of the earliest surviving texts of Sappho. Inscribed on a terracotta pot, now broken, it is a copy of Sappho's Prayer to Aphrodite. Margaret Williamson. 1995. *Sappho's Immortal Daughters*, p. 57.

7 *gossiping*. Women gossip when we share news and important information. Like many words associated with women it has pejorative uses. The word "gossip" comes from "gob sibb", "sibb" refers to kin, relation, special friend, someone with whom you spend time and are close to. *Gossip* is also the name of a lesbian magazine published in England by Onlywomen Press in the 1980s.

8 *cafes*. A great deal of lesbian life takes place in cafes. Wherever there are lesbian communities, there are cafes.

firenze

in honour of Jacqui Stockdale's painting

two women[1] dream of a third who is setting off on a journey she carries an ancient rose[2] and rides a flying horse[3] this is a floating world solid as brick[4] immaterial as a dream above is the sound of beating the shadow of a wing over my bare head

I twist her hair in ritual[5] I twist it into a turban I weave scarves through it she winds plaits of hair around my head we dream of a world that is lost a world we make manifest

in Firenze[6] we walk the narrow streets some of us bear tattoos on our arms necks buttocks backs sculpted women disembodied busts float

we traverse virtual architectures in the doorways women converse as they always have gossiping[7] some sip coffee in outdoor cafes[8] one leans on elbows gazing into the eyes of another she leans and speaks to the woman at the neighbouring table they laugh red geraniums bloom in a window box and some solitary woman waters them daily

behind arched windows women live out the scenes of love and loss framed by the ancient architraves the columned

9 *secret meetings*. There are many places where lesbianism is still outlawed. The shadowless informant is never far away in these places.

10 *the bridge making it their home*. The bridge is a between place, a place where connections are made or unmade. Gloria Anzaldúa refers to it as "*nepantla*, a Nahuatl word meaning *tierra entre medio*" in her preface "(Un)natural bridges, (Un)safe spaces" which opens the anthology *This Bridge We Call Home: Radical Visions for Transformation* (2002), p. 1.

11 *trapped souls*. A reference to Monique Wittig's vision of Heaven, Purgatory and Hell in *Across the Acheron*.

12 *breads high tin loaves and baguettes*. Judy Grahn explores the bread metaphor in *The Work of a Common Woman* (1978).

13 *Boston*. "A Boston marriage is an affectional, but non-sexual" relationship between two women. See Kay Turner. 1996. *Dear Sappho: A Legacy of Lesbian Love Letters, 1996*. p. 14. For a longer treatment see Lillian Faderman's *Surpassing the Love of Men*, pp. 178-203.

14 *butterfly*. "Blue butterfly morning glory heart". These are the first and last words of a piece by Jeffner Allen, "Passion in the Gardens of Delight". In Judith Barrington (Ed.). 1991. *An Intimate Wilderness*, pp. 279-283. "You are present at the ceremony of the vulvas lost and found … The vulvas are represented by blue yellow green black violet red butterflies, their bodies are the clitorises, their wings are the labia, their fluttering represents the throbbing of the vulvas." Monique Wittig, 1975. *The Lesbian Body*, p. 135-6.

15 *fruit and vegetables*. Melbourne playwright, Sara Hardy, has written "Queer Fruit", a play which draws on the fruity side of lesbian relationships and has a recurring chant: "Queer fruit, mixed with Time, / Queer time, dangerous pleasure, / Queer, bi, gay, lesbian, tranni, / Queer fruit for so many."

16 *Ibu women*. The Ibu of Nigeria fought the Women's War of 1929 against the British colonialists with pots and pans. For more on this see Flora Nwapa's *Cassava Song and Rice Song*, 1986. As M. Jacqui Alexander reminds us, the Ibu (also known as Ibo) were captured and transported as slaves to the Georgia Sea Islands. M. Jacqui Alexander. 2002. "Remembering *This Bridge*, Remembering Ourselves: Yearning, Memory and Desire." *This Bridge We Call Home*, pp. 81-103.

porticos are chosen for secret meetings[9] plots are made betrayals are formulated

huge potted plants stand on the verandahs where the shadowless woman and her companion hide in the curves of the bridge making it their home[10]

beyond are the curling stairways which lead endlessly up and down an infinite cycle the upward stair finishes abruptly arriving at no floor no destination so some poor trapped souls[11] progress nowhere although they are in constant motion in pairs some travel to the Piazzale Michelangelo to admire the patterns of the red slate rooves of this city

the observer is drawn to the alleyways where market stalls pull in a constant stream of customers the women sell gold sandalwood books and kohl

old women sell handbaked breads woven like plaited hair flat breads high tin loaves and baguettes[12] sit side by side with Boston buns[13] and butterfly[14] cakes

others sell fruits and vegetables[15] picked fresh pickled or preserved and then there are the pots and pans such as the Ibu women[16] used defending themselves from violence and from hunger

17 *hatted*. Women have often gone scarved or hatted in public places, sometimes for safety, sometimes in disguise. On other occasions the wearing of a hat has been the beginning of a love affair. Sylvia Beach and Adrienne Monnier attribute their relationship to a hat. They met one day when Sylvia Beach was leaving Shakespeare and Co, the Paris bookstore run by Adrienne Monnier. A gust of wind blew Sylvia's hat into the street. Adrienne rescued the hat, and their eyes met as she returned it to Sylvia. I wonder if this might be the source for Gertrude Stein's lines: "I love my love with a dress and a hat / I love my love and not with this or with that / I love my love with a y because she is my bride / I love her with a d because she is my love beside" "Before the Flowers of Friendship Faded Friendship Faded". In Gertrude Stein. 1971. *Look at Me Now and Here I Am*, p. 286. For a mystery lesbian ghost story centred on hats see Merrilee Moss. 2001. *Fedora Walks*.

18 *masked abandon*. A reference to the Carnivale of Venice and other places. In opera such masked reveries are often the site of lesbian connection.

19 *bougainvillea*. See Donna McSkimming. 1986. *Beware the Bougainvillea*, pp. 8-9. The bougainvillea is not the threat, but rather the group of unknown men in a restaurant in "A Fairy Tale", pp. 21-22.

20 *Sissinghurst*. Vita Sackville-West's famous garden in England. It is a place of pilgrimage for many contemporary lesbians.

21 *paradise*. Paradise was originally a walled garden, a place of retreat. Jeffner Allen writes: "The delights of touch and tongue abound when paradise is lost." Jeffner Allen. 1991. "Passion in the Gardens of Delight", p. 281. Monique Wittig, on the other hand, equates paradise with new love. Paradise is contrasted with the hell of heterosexuality and its commodification and violence in *Across the Acheron*.

the cupola floats like a giant balloon blooming behind the buildings under the dome voices rise billowing clouds of sound waft in the great space above the hatted heads[17]

in the square in front of the cathedral the art of daily life proceeds some play politics and the arts annually we indulge in a masked abandon[18] we know one another only by our gait our hands our body shape for our faces have been covered with masks of all kinds masks carved from wood moulded with plaster masks decorated with paints of cerise turquoise and tangerine with coloured feathers flowers in season and ribbons streaming in the wind like cobras swaying to the sounds of an Indian flute

green tendrils poke between cobblestones in spring a wall is covered in bougainvillea[19] my lover and I kiss under those walls whether covered in climbing roses or cultivated creepers just as others have kissed beneath the purple spills of Sissinghurst[20] or in some ancient time beneath the hanging gardens of Babylon there we find paradise[21] there we lose it

[illegible]

22 *familiars*. Animals kept by those accused of witchcraft during the men's renaissance were referred to as familiars. Many women burned as witches were women living apart from men.

we share our home with dogs cats birds rats and other familiars[22] she and I cultivate ourselves also plants and children who peek through holes in canvases pretending to be from another world believing they are unseen by us I watch as the pupil moves across the eye

the sky shines behind the cupola and she and I argue about whether it has a flag flying from the apex we are all touched by patterns pathways mazes or the motion of an electron across our shoulders our diaphragms move without effort whereas the women in platform shoes stumble as they progress

phantoms press up against us we move back into the alleyways to find shelter we climb the stairs leading to the verandahs into the houses framed by arched windows we draw the curtains pull off our scarves unwind our hair retreat into the inner sanctum and from time to time we water the geraniums in the window box

1 *opening night*. The performance was by the Performing Older Women's Circus (POW Circus) established in Melbourne in 1995. Maureen (Maurs) O'Connor was a founding member. She was also a fine and funny clown and head techie until the end of 1997. Maureen's life is recorded by Jean Taylor in *The C-Word* (2000).

2 *querent*. The theme for the 1998 show was tarot. The performers used these images to explore different aspects of the cards. Shuffle, cut, stack. Images from the POW deck. Over the Top. "Over the Top with Tarot" was performed from 24 to 26 September 1998 at the Pit Theatre, Footscray Community Arts Centre.

3 *cathedral*. A double balance in which the base lies on her back with legs vertical. The flyer places her head between the feet, holding hands with the base and she springs into an inverted position on the base's feet.

4 *highest point*. The highest point in the show was an inverted hanging position in the space between two trapezes. The invert and the between space both represent lesbian existence.

5 *Fool*. The first and final card in the Tarot pack. It represents creativity and openness to life which comes with wisdom. As a clown, Maurs was more than familiar with the Fool. Indeed, lesbians take to clowning with great relish. Having discarded conventional women's roles, it is relatively easy to take the next step and to act out unrestrained impulses which most would not dream of doing. Maurs' clown self was shy, unprepossessing, with a timid walk, and facial expressions which ranged from shame to sheer joy. One finds examples of clowning and humour from figures in Greek literature such as Baubo, who lifted her skirts and made the goddess Demeter laugh again.

death

for Maureen O'Connor

it is midnight time to gather around your death you sit on the couch where you sat just last week when we talked the lambskin covers your now-thin shoulders your lesbians-are-everywhere T-shirt sags where flesh has faded

each performs her own private ritual caressing your hands your knees your breathless cheeks each communes with her own silences death is not easy it raises monsters and fears it reminds us of mortality of fragility

Roisín curls into your body including you in her conversation she has been with death many times and is not cowed by her

after you died Maria came to collect your brown felt hat your clowning hat with its sunflower it sat upon the speaker as we performed for the opening-night audience and for you[1]

we are each a querent[2] we each take journeys to death on that night an invisible hand pulled me into a cathedral[3] and as I reached the highest point[4] I muttered to myself this one's for you it was the Fool[5] of course

6 *purple flowers*. Purple flowers have a long association with lesbians. From violets, amaranth, hyacinth, narcissus, purple flowers have been worn to indicate that one does not intend to marry. For more on this see Judy Grahn. 1984. *Another Mother Tongue*, p. 8. Purple also indicates a transformative state, the μεταξυ, the in-between, a state familiar to lesbians.

7 *labrys*. The labrys, (Gr. λαβρυσ) is the double axe which was used in Minoan Crete. Lesbians took up the symbol as representing our sexuality during the 1970s. The labrys in the Minoan era was associated with women. Symbolic connections have been made between the labrys, the butterfly and women's genitalia. Unfortunately, as with many ancient symbols, it has also been used for fascist purposes. Mussolini used the symbol of the double axe, and in Italy today it still carries fascist connotations.

8 *waiting*. Death is infinitely patient, as The Black Piglet discovers in Suniti Namjoshi's *Building Babel*, pp. 14-16.

9 *Lethe*. Lethe, "forgetting" looms large for lesbians who are forgotten or written out of history. Forgetting can come from the fog of complacency.

we stand in the cold gathering small purple flowers[6] from the garden I place the seven-petalled bloom on your body my hands shaped like the butterfly the soul the labrys[7] we sing life being what it is we turn this into theatre forming an archway farewelling you circling the car here to take you away from us

none of us knows how to die death comes again and again a stalker forever in pursuit the chase is over for some before we know it's begun for others death visits at every opportunity at dinner parties and dances or she is caught standing silently beside the bed of a loved one waiting waiting[8]

once I watched as death gentled her next subject into a boat she took up the oars rowed into the fog leaving me listening to the lapping waves of the Lethe[9]

1 *long leather boots*. Photographs of Vita Sackville-West in her Sissinghurst garden show her leaning up against a wooden paling fence wearing high leather boots. The photograph of Edna Walling that opens chapter one of Sara Hardy's biography, depicts her in jodhpurs and long boots. See *The Unusual Life of Edna Walling* (2005).

2 *narrow beds*. Anchee Min in *Red Azalea* (1994) tells the story of how she is sent to Red Fire Farm to work with the peasants. There on the farm she meets Yan, the company leader. Her first impressions of Yan as powerful, as someone not to be messed with are followed by a deepening respect and love for this woman who "... was famous for her iron shoulders ... carrying over a hundred and sixty pounds in two hods hanging from a shoulder pole." Anchee Min begins to emulate Yan; she tries to work as fast as her, and Yan begins to reward her. As Anchee Min's awareness of her sexuality grows, she falls more and more deeply in love with Yan. Soon she begins to find out other things about Yan, and it is not long before they are sharing the same narrow bed.

3 *golden threads*. Golden Threads is a USA-based contact publication for older and mid-life lesbians. Older lesbians are often faced with the assumption that lesbianism is a young woman's lifestyle choice. In fact, a significant number of women wait until their children have left home before deciding to act on their feelings for women. Jennifer Kelly explores how lesbians at menopause – because of expectations within the lesbian community about body image and the aging body – experience it in significantly different ways. See *Zest for Life* (2005).

4 *salt of the earth*. According to Barbara Walker, salt of the earth was a Semitic metaphor applied to seers. And "Cabalistic tradition suggests that the biblical Lot's wife was really a form of the Triple Goddess. Hebrew MLH "salt" is a sacred word because its numerical value is that of God's name of power YHWH, multiplied three times." *The Woman's Encyclopedia of Myths and Secrets*, p. 887.

5 *husbandry*. The original meaning of "to husband" is farm work to win the hand of a woman. Women also worked farms and wooed women, cross-dressing until such time as a woman revealed herself. There are many stories of such women, particularly farm workers. Eve Langley's *The Pea Pickers* (1942) includes cross-dressing women, and Eve Langley herself had a history of cross-dressing. Lesbian usage of the word "husband" has a long history. Eliza Raine writing to Anne Lister in 1806 refers to Anne as "my husband". Jill Liddington. 1998. *Female Fortune: Land Gender and Authority, The Anne Lister Diaries and Other Writings, 1833-36*, p. 15.

6 *raised cows*. The Ladies of Llangollen, Eleanor Butler and Sarah Ponsonby, eloped in 1778, set up in a cottage together and raised a cow, Margaret Ponsonby. For more on the Ladies see Elizabeth Mavor. 1973. *The Ladies of Llangollen: A Study of Romantic Friendship*. Unfortunately Mavor's book plays down the lesbian sexuality of this pair. Also see Lillian Faderman. 1981. *Surpassing the Love of Men*, pp. 75-81.

7 *everyday lesbian separatists*. Suniti Namjoshi's wonderfully irreverent tale about migration and cultural difference, *The Conversations of Cow*, has as its central character Bhadravati, a Brahmin cow who strikes up a friendship with Suniti, the narrator. Bhadravati, on taking her new friend, Suniti, to visit friends in the country remarks, "I ought to tell you, Cow informs me, 'that this is a Self-Sustaining Community of Lesbian Cows.' I scrutinise Cow. So, Cow and I have something in common." Suniti Namjoshi. 1985. *The Conversations of Cow*, pp. 17-18.

gumboots and goblin fruit

we pull on gumboots long leather boots[1] riding boots work boots walk barefooted to the field drive the tractor the ute the four-wheel-drive the motor bike we ride horses donkeys mules camels and llamas just to get to our fields

we are farmers some because we were born to it others because we chose it

Xiaolin farms under duress sent to work beside the peasants she finds her pleasure in narrow beds[2] in China we tend mulberry trees and farm silk worms the golden threads[3] binding us together around the world we are salt of the earth[4]

we excel in husbandry[5] many of us have raised cows[6] we make pets of them call them by name some of these cows have been everyday lesbian separatists[7] not cowed by

8 *Bhadravati Boudicca Cowslip Sybilla*. The names of some of the cows in the "Self Sustaining Community of Lesbian Cows".

9 *Cow*. Gertrude Stein's long poem, *Lifting Belly*, explores the language of lesbian sexuality, creating a whole new range of metaphors for lesbians. She writes: "Twenty six. / And counted. / And counted deliberately. / This is not as difficult as it seems. / Lifting belly is so strange / And quick. / Lifting belly in a minute. / Lifting belly in a minute now. / In a minute. /Not to-day. / No not to-day. / Can you swim. / Lifting belly can perform aquatics. / Lifting belly is astonishing. / Lifting belly for me. / Come together." In Gertrude Stein. 1989. *Lifting Belly*, pp. 53-4. For more on the cow metaphor see Rebecca Mark's introduction, especially p. xxxi. In 1975, there was a lesbian newsletter in Columbus, Ohio, called The Purple Cow. This information appeared in a listing of lesbian resources in Gina Covina and Laurel Galana (Eds.). 1975. *The Lesbian Reader*, p. 246.

10 *Jumped over the moon*. The songs *Bessie* (1996) and *The Mystery at Ogwen's Farm* (1981) are both by Jane Siberry and can be found on *The Jane Siberry Anthology*. Originally produced by Sheeba. If Mother Goose Stories are stories about a great goddess, then perhaps the story of the cow jumping over the moon could be read as a story about the great orgasm of a goddess!

11 *Saraswati*. Hindu goddess of writing. It is possible to connect philologically the names Saraswati and Sappho. See "India Sutra", this collection. The Saraswati River is an invisible underground river and, therefore, shares some of the attributes of lesbian existence.

12 *geese and wet hens*. "Watch us – mother hens, slick chicks, silly geese, all of us – after centuries of being cooped up, centuries of brooding in our roosts, we're finally going to spread our wings." Jovette Marchessault. 1983. *The Saga of the Wet Hens*. p. 128. Marchessault goes on to invoke the history of women who have challenged the status quo, to call up their spirit of rebellion.

13 *red beaked black swans*. "I am no Leda ... // I am moved / to transformation / by another // black feathered, / red beaked / female swan." Leda. Susan Hawthorne. In Susan Hawthorne, Cathie Dunsford, and Susan Sayer (Eds.). 1997. *Car Maintenance, Explosives and Love and Other Contemporary Lesbian Writings*, p. 129. The black swan existed in spite of the protestations of scientists and logicians that such a thing could not be. It was, they said, unnatural and impossible.

14 *gobbling*. Christina Rosetti uses the word "goblin" to great effect in her long poem, "Goblin Market". The old meanings of the word "gob" are interesting, ranging across mouth (as in shut your gob, or the rather large lollies called gob-stoppers), language (as in the gift of the gab), to talk incessantly, (as in gabble). To gobble, means to swallow noisily, rather like a turkey. The word "gob" was in much more frequent use in 1862 when Christina Rosetti published her poem. "Goblin pulp and goblin dew" were the words which prompted these thoughts, but there are other references in the poem which are even more suggestive of lesbian sexuality. "Did you miss me? / Come and kiss me. / Never mind my bruises, / Hug me, kiss me, suck my juices / squeezed from goblin fruits for you, / Goblin pulp and goblin dew. / Eat me, drink me, love me; / Laura, make much of me." Christina Rosetti. 1994. *Goblin Market and other poems*, p. 13.

15 *tree-climbing workshops*. An ideal profession for lesbian tomboys who have a penchant for climbing trees, just like the apple pickers of Sappho's time.

amazons Margaret Bhadravati Boudicca Cowslip Sybilla[8] or just plain old Cow[9] then there's Bessie the flying cow the cow who jumped over the moon[10] in a paroxysm of pleasure

it's a riparian existence Saraswati[11] flowing beneath us another underground world invisible like us generating surface flow petals thrown into the water swirl and spin eddying downstream

ducks geese and wet hens[12] live in our coops they guard us and befriend us each day we gather eggs waiting and listening for the crowing which heralds the newest egg the newest world my best friends are ducks Radclyffe and Alice I follow mother goose around the yard with her thirteen goslings in train only eleven return I go in search of the missing two find them in fence holes next to the paddock nearby in the wetlands red-beaked black swans[13] stretch their legs as they step on to the muddy water's edge further north the cassowary's blue head bobs in and out of sight the mother lays the egg but then dispenses child care to the males' wing

in the parched chook run turkeys gobble their throats wobbling swallowing words gobbling[14] half words

the one we call Monkey runs tree-climbing workshops[15] she works in the trees and has learnt to spread her weight

16 *memory and the goddess of love*. Reference is often made in Sappho's poems to Aphrodite, the goddess of love, and to Mnemosyne, the muse of memory.

17 *grass*. Sappho and her great poetic colleague, Anonymous, have both referred to grass and the delights of nature in their poems. "A Woman's Song: To Her Indifferent Lover" written in Latin in the eleventh century includes these lines: "*Tu saltim, Veris gratia / exaudi et considera / frondes, flores et gramina; / nam mea languet anima*". Gillian Spragg has translated this poem and the verse reads: "You, at least, for the spring's sake, / listen, and give your mind / to the flowers, the leaves, the grasses; / my spirit pines". See the Babel Building Site on the internet at: http://www.spinifexpress.com.au/bb/piglet/somewind.htm. Gillian Spragg has also translated, Sappho's Fragment 31. Spragg's translation goes as follows: "cold sweat pours down me, and in every part / shuddering grips me; / I am paler than summer grass, / and seem to myself to be at the point of death". Gillian Spragg. "Divine Visitations; Sappho's Poetry of Love". In Elaine Hobby and Chris White (Eds.). 1991. *What Lesbians Do in Books*, p.55. See my poem "Seized: Variations on Sappho's Fragment 31". In Susan Hawthorne. 1999. *Bird*, pp. 71-74.

18 *Basket*. Gertrude Stein had a series of dogs, all called Basket.

19 *suck at mangoes*. Cathie Dunsford describes how to eat mango Pacific style in *The Journey Home / Te Haerenga Kainga* (1997), p. 108.

20 *pineapples bananas*. Jordan, in *Sexing the Cherry* by Jeanette Winterson (1989), goes in search of such fruits and the paradise they represent.

21 *savour its juices*. "Hugged her and kissed her: / Squeezed and caressed her: / Stretched up their dishes, / Panniers and plates: / "look at our apples / Russet and dun, / Bob at our cherries, / Bite at our peaches, / Citrons and dates, / Grapes for the asking, / Pears red with basking / out in the sun, / Plum on their twigs; / pluck them and suck them, / Pomegranates, figs." Christina Rosetti. 1994. *Goblin Market and other poems*, p. 10. This passage is replete with sexual innuendo, with so many of these fruits being associated with women's sexuality.

with the assistance of harnesses and pulleys she can go anywhere up or down across and around the young ones clamour to be in her classes they disappear into the canopies of the very highest trees they can be heard whispering among the branches which hang low over the river

one has learnt the art of climbing a vertical trunk aided only by a strip of rag and her own loose limbs she retrieves coconuts tossing them to catchers below

in the orchards we grow peaches and pears plucking them in our fingers the apple trees are for climbing each year a prize goes to the one who can reach the highest apple we do this in memory of Sappho sitting on the highest branch invoking memory and the goddess of love[16]

in the tree's shade lovers loll picnic hampers filled with avocadoes and a bottle of wine the grass[17] is soft and green they share their leftovers with the dog Basket[18]

we suck at mangoes[19] straight off the tree the ground is strewn with those ripened too early for our touch

among us are voyagers who go in search of pineapples bananas[20] custard apples and other joys of the mouth the taste buds we caress each peach as it is pulled from the tree we savour its juices[21] on hot days we lick our lips after

22 *lemon*. In Australia lesbians are referred to as lemons. In 2001 Auberon Waugh derisively called the Orange Prize for Fiction, the Lemon Award. *Sunday Age, Agenda*, 8 July 2001. p. 10. Elizabeth Ashburn's book *Lesbian Art: An encounter with power* (1996) has on its cover an image of twelve lemons. The cover is a detail from a work by Koori artist, Rea. *Lemons 1*. C-type photograph. 40 x 100 cm, 1994.

23 *cabbages*. Lesbians, it is said, "are born today from ear to ear" for as Monique Wittig and Sande Zeig point out, "the atrocious mutilations once suffered by the newborn when their cabbages were accidentally cut are thus avoided." *Lesbian Peoples* (1979), p. 49.

24 *potatoes*. "Potatoes are a lot like lesbians. They're all the same and they're all different." Bode Noonan, 1986. *Red Beans and Rice*. Cited in Rosemary Silva. (Ed.) 1993. *Lesbian Quotations*, p. 19.

25 *Med*. Mad Med is a character in Suniti Namjoshi's *Building Babel* (1996). Many lesbians have been labelled mad; many have suffered incarceration and ill-treatment as a result.

26 *black sheep*. Lesbians and other rebellious women have often been labelled as black sheep of the family, the oddity, the marked one. This, of course, assumes a white norm.

27 *spin*. Spinsters and lesbians are often one and the same. They spin thread or tales, just as the Norns and the Fates of legend did. The -ster ending on many surnames indicates a profession of women, a good proportion of these women pursuing independent means were single or were lesbians. Among the professions suggested by this suffix are: spinsters (spinners), websters (weavers), baxters (bakers), sisters (nuns, nurses). More unusual words, kempster (a female wool comber), huckster (a seller of smallgoods) and dempster (a judge, or deemer) can be found. There are some puzzling words such as: monster (although Robin Morgan's poem suggests this might not be surprising; youngster (but it is a person without power); more puzzling perhaps is gangster, but a gangster is a person without a gang, without the power of numbers. In Sigrid Undset's novel, *Kristin Lavransdatter* (1951) the word moster, mother's sister, is used.

28 *wool*. Wool was the foundation of wealth for the Listers of Shibden Hall. Anne Lister, the best-documented lesbian of the nineteenth century, was a beneficiary of this wealth. See Jill Liddington. 1998. *Female Fortune*, p. 15.

sipping at lemons[22] relishing the sweetness of the after taste on our lips on our tongue we wonder whether the poor lemon is really so impossible to eat

the market gardens are rich in produce we carry the fruit in bags over our shoulders Christina consorts with goblins elves and pixies sharing the pear the apple the cherry the juices running you'll find no offspring sheltering under cabbages[23] you'll find only potatoes[24] ripe tomatoes root vegetables zucchini the many-headed cauliflower and broccoli

on the plains Elizabeth and Medea raise sheep last season I was there assisting as we walked the paddock it was Med[25] who spotted the ewe in trouble a breech birth the legs emerging first black legs it's one of us we cheered as the black sheep[26] came into the world we raised it on a bottle once there was a Cyclops lamb with a single eye in the centre of its forehead

as midwinter passes its nadir we shear and spin[27] the wool[28] into yarn for next winter's cold in the mountains of Tibet we raise blue sheep keeping the wolves at bay with our wild voices long ago in Colchis we worshipped the ewe her golden fleece bringing us wealth and luck

1 *sea*. Bonnie Zimmerman's literary analysis of mostly American lesbian fiction puts the sea at the centre. *The Safe Sea of Women: Lesbian Fiction 1969-1989* (1990).

2 *takatapui*. This is a word used by some Maori lesbians to describe their sexuality.

3 *on islands lesbians thrive*. Monique Wittig and Sande Zeig refer to the migrations to islands by lesbians. They write: "In large numbers the companion lovers of the Glorious Age have started looking for islands. Most have chosen islands where the great tropical rainforests continue to grow. These islands form a belt on both sides of the equator." *Lesbian Peoples*. (1979), p. 85. In the Author's Note to *The Lesbian Body*, 1975, Wittig writes: "We already have our islets, our islands." p. 9.

4 *Lesbos*. Sappho lived on the island of Lesbos in the seventh century BCE. "… all the lesbians or companion lovers go there one day." *Lesbian Peoples* (1979), p. 97.

5 *Capri*. Wealthy lesbians of the 1920s holidayed on Capri. Among them, artist Romaine Brooks, who in 1918 bought Villa Cercola. Faith Compton Mackenzie wrote of her: "A heat wave, hot even for Capri in August, sent temperatures up. Feverish bouquets of exhausted blooms lay about the big studio, letters and invites strewed her desk, ignored for the most part, while she, wrapped in her cloak, would wander down to the town as the evening cooled and sit in the darkest corner of Morgano's Café terrace, maddeningly remote and provocative." Meryle Secrest. 1976. *Between Me and Life: A Biography of Romaine Brooks*, p. 285.

6 *Malta*. Around 4500 years ago huge temples were built on the island of Malta. The Hypogeum of Hal Saflieni has been hewn from the soft limestone and descends several stories below ground. A place of burial and worship, with some 7000 bodies found there, the shape of the Hypogeum resembles ancient figurines of women. For this reason, it is a place of pilgrimage for some lesbians. Cristina Biaggi. 1994. *Habitations of the Great Goddess*.

7 *Crete*. The home of the ancient Minoan civilisation, Crete has become a favoured destination for many lesbians in search of a culture in which women were at least equal with men. Of great appeal to many lesbians are the stories of the labyrinth and the bull leapers. Dorothy Porter writes of the athleticism and sexuality of bull-leaping. Dorothy Porter. 1996. *Crete*, p. 26. The word labyrinth is related to labrys, the double axe, a powerful lesbian symbol of the 1970s. As noted previously, Mussolini's Fascists also used the double axe as their symbol, resulting in an understandably ambivalent attitude towards the labrys in some quarters.

8 *St Croix*. Not in the image of the Mediterranean islands, St Croix in the Caribbean became the island retreat of Audre Lorde. She died there in 1992. See Alexis de Veaux. 2004. *Warrior Poet: A Biography of Audre Lorde.* The sad irony is that in many Caribbean islands – including the Bahamas, Trinidad and Tobago, Antigua and Barbuda, Barbados – it is illegal to be a lesbian. I wonder how many tourist lesbians are arrested and jailed, or is it only aimed at locals?

9 *Fiji*. Lesbian travel agencies, such as Silke's operating out of Sydney, have organised lesbian weeks at a resort in Fiji. Like the Caribbean, the Fiji and Pacific islands are running the risk of becoming exoticised islands for rich western lesbians.

10 *Isla Mujeres*. Off the coast of Mexico, these islands of women inspire lesbians to travel in the hope of finding paradise. Of course paradise is never that easy to find even in a name as promising as this.

amphibious lips

we tuck hibiscus behind our ears and dance for the visitors lesbians in grass skirts is how we are billed we dance and sing and when we finish we place a garland of flowers over the head of a chosen one

the sound of the sea[1] breaking on a coral reef is in our ears we lie in a rattan-woven walled hut the ceiling made of bamboo and a thatched roof no nails have been used in its construction

on other islands women walk on fire dive for fish off the coral shelf tumble three hundred and sixty degrees in that magic underwater world she strokes the Maori wrasse with its tattooed gills dances with grouper at the cod hole falls without landing on the sand below some climb coconut palms or pluck oysters from their beds among them are those who are called takatapui[2]

on islands lesbians thrive[3] our known origins our culture and dreams are islands Lesbos[4] Capri[5] Malta[6] Crete[7] St Croix[8] Fiji[9] Isla Mujeres[10]

11 *casting off*. See Lara Fergus. 2005. "Lifeboat".

12 *the seven sisters*. Also known as the Pleiades. There is much mythology centred on this star cluster. Many peoples have used the Pleiades as a calendar or as a guide in navigation. Sappho wrote of the Pleiades in one of her Fragments "The moon and the Pleiades have set / the night is half gone / hours pass / still I sleep alone." Translation Susan Hawthorne. 1984. For more on the Pleiades, see Munya Andrews. 2004. *The Seven Sisters of the Pleiades: Stories from around the World*.

13 *pirates*. Famous among historical pirates are Mary Read (b. 1690) and Anne Bonney (fl. 1718), both of whom cross-dressed as men and are said to have fallen for one another. As happens in the lives of some lesbians, they are said to have later married and been condemned to hang. Mary Read died of a fever, and Anne Bonney disappeared from the history books.

14 *lighthouse*. A reference to Virginia Woolf's *To the Lighthouse* (1990), whose main character, artist Lily Briscoe, herself became the central focus of the autobiography of artist, Mary Meigs. 1981. *Lily Briscoe: A Self Portrait*. Jeanette Winterson's *Lighhousekeeping* (2005) is also a nod in the direction of Virginia Woolf. The suggestion is that whoever set out to the lighthouse is now installed there. Artist, Suzanne Bellamy's Lily Briscoe Series, 1999 was reproduced in *The Australian's Review of Books*, pp. 3-5, and 30.

15 *curve of a breast*. "The curve of your breast is like the curve / of a wave: look, held, caught, each instant / caught, the wave tipping over and we in our bower, / the two of us sheltered, my hands on your thighs, / your body, your back, my mouth on your mouth / in the hollows of your jaws and your head / nuzzling my breasts. And the wave above us is / folding over now, folding and laughing. Will you / take to the sea, my darling?" From "Well, then let slip the masks." Suniti Namjoshi and Gillian Hanscombe. 1986. *Flesh and Paper*, p. 19.

16 *none of us can walk straight*. Lesbian writers have reflected on the impossibility of straight lines, straight thinking. "The waves are curved lines on a sphere (earth) which moves in a spiral around a central point (the sun) which whirls through another spiral (the galaxy) which is part of an infinite boundless universal spiral. So to talk about the shortest distance between two points as a straight line is ludicrous. Nothing from the smallest particle to the galactic arms moves in a straight line." Susan Hawthorne. 1992. *The Falling Woman*. p. 200. Also see Monique Wittig, 1992. *The Straight Mind and Other Essays*.

17 *the waves break on the shore*. The last sentence of Virginia Woolf's novel *The Waves* is: "The waves broke on the shore." Virginia Woolf. 1969. *The Waves*, p. 256.

18 *wreck*. Lesbian lives are real, and the reality often bears little resemblance to the mythology surrounding lesbian existence. It is, as Adrienne Rich writes: "the wreck and not the story of the wreck / the thing itself and not the myth", "Diving into the Wreck", 1973. *Diving into the Wreck*, p. 23.

we take our boats casting off[11] into unfathomable depths could paradise be a watery realm? will we find safe passage? we are rowing sailing drifting across the seas navigating by the stars following the path of the seven sisters[12] we climb the fo'castle like pirates[13] search for hidden treasure on unmarked islands peering out across the waves

at night we trace our futures in the stars measuring the angles with our eyes we catch sight of the lighthouse[14] and steer towards it

the waves carry us the curve of each wave like the curve of a breast[15] walking in circles in sways in curves none of us can walk straight[16] we walk over the heave of the ocean the body rising in arcs even the bones moving in circles

as the waves break on the shore[17] we dive under them another underworld to explore where giant clams lazily open velvet lips bêche du mer slump into the sand and fish flick in and out of peripheral vision

I breathe out and sink to the bottom I'm waiting for the big one reef shark octopus stingray or some transparent polyp prepared to take it front on my eyes are stunned to staring and the wreck[18] lies nearby

19 *corals*. "Silently we are cementing our lives / As a coral reef is built / Blossoming into iridescence / Providing homes for wandering Angel fish / and other bits of beauty." Rita Mae Brown. 1974. *The Hand that Cradles the Rock*, p. 38.

20 *amphibians*. "Lesbians have become cultural amphibians." Susan Hawthorne, Cathie Dunsford and Susan Sayer (Eds.). 1997. *Car Maintenance, Explosives and Love and Other Contemporary Lesbian Writings*, p. x. A reference to the dual cultural life lived by lesbians. Many lesbians live a multiple cultural life, inhabiting a variety of cultural domains. Janice Raymond's "two sights-seeing" reflects a similar concept. See Janice Raymond. 1986. *A Passion for Friends: Toward a Philosophy of Female Affection*, pp. 203-241.

21 *white horses*. Finola Moorhead, writes of Ursula, the surfer: "the sea is her great mirror. The sea is as she is inside, behind the shell of appearance, beyond the unopened door of her hymen." *Remember the Tarantella*, 1987, pp. 16-17. Ursula is probably the first lesbian surfer in Australian literature. Lesbian sexuality has often been linked with horse riding. Riding the white horses of the surf is simply a new variation on an old theme.

22 *mouth*. The Greek word for mouth "stoma" (Gr. στομα) refers to the mouth and lips, as well as to the vagina. For lesbians, the mouth has a multidimensional importance as the site of both speech and sexual desire.

23 *a figure on a ship's deck*. It was on a ship's deck near Corfu that H.D. had a vision which was to influence her poetry for many years. See H.D.'s *Tribute to Freud* (1974).

24 *nautilus*. "A pink chambered nautilus / Her womb whispers songs of the sea / Oh, yes / Say yes / And come make love with me." Rita Mae Brown. 1973. *Songs to a Handsome Woman*, p. 19. Suzanne Bellamy, an Australian porcelain artist began in the late 1970s to make vulval figurines in the shapes of shells. Her work is displayed in lesbian households around the country, as well as in collections elsewhere.

some days we float above corals[19] formed like brains trees mushrooms and surreal sculptures the seaweed follows in our wake when we emerge our masks and flippers turn us into aliens but we are amphibians[20] our breathing returns to oxygen mixed with nitrogen the water runs down our bodies making them gleam in the late afternoon sun

at daybreak we surf inside the reef's edge riding white horses[21] surfboards tyres through the foaming spume you decide to try water skiing and stand on the second attempt your trapezoids strong from work your body shape not determined by fashion

there are islands where secrets are embedded in the rocks in the shape of the coastline where the sweet waters mix with the sea myriad birds live near the mouth[22] visiting in cycles bringing culture

and we too circle like a figure on a ship's deck[23] through to the final place where we are buried surrounded by circles of rocks and trees in the evenings you and I walk the foreshore searching out the shell of a nautilus[24]

25 *molluscs*. "I could tell // how you took my fingers / into your mouth and I was hungry / to suck your mollusc tongue / coated musk rich and salty" Donna McSkimming. "Ocean Travelling" In *Three's Company*. (1992).

26 *anemones*. "Are there many things in this cool-hearted world so utterly exquisite as the pure love of one woman for another. // And so do I remember my one friend, the anemone lady – and think often about her with passionate love." Mary MacLane (d.1921). In *The Art of Lesbian Love*, p. 50. For more on Mary MacLane see Lillian Faderman. 1981. *Surpassing the Love of Men*, pp. 299-300.

27 *Uṣas*. For a lesbian perspective on the story of Uṣas, see Giti Thadani. 1996. *Sakhiyani*, pp. 33-38. Her relationship to Greek Aphrodite is explored in Susan Hawthorne. 1982. *The Homeric Hymns to Demeter and Aphrodite*.

we build fires on the beach cooking the feasts of the sea we break open the shell fish drawing their flesh into ours we tongue molluscs[25] we pop seaweed with our fingers and our tongues are like anemones[26] seeking refuge between rocks between thighs

night wanes and gold-stranded Aphrodite rises over the mirror sea casting glances at Uṣas[27] her sister pre-Homeric and pre-Vedic they raise a storm kicking up their heels in phantasmagorical flight over the many-maned sea these mares will not be stolen the stampede picks up pace Pegasus and every unicorn or magical mare leaps and is airborne

1 *the land*. In a very different landscape Vita Sackville-West wrote two long poems, *The Land* (1926) and *The Garden* (1946). See Vita Sackville-West. 1989. *The Land and The Garden*.

2 *the known world*. The known world is rarely a lesbian world. Monique Wittig explores the possibility of a Virgilian journey into unknown worlds in *Across the Acheron*. 1987.

3 *kelpie*. Old Scots for water spirit, kelpies in Australia are working sheepdogs. For a twist on the Scottish tale, see Cathie Dunsford. 2001. *Song of the Selkies*.

4 *Olga*. A character from *The Falling Woman*. 1992. She accompanies Estella on a desert journey. The desert journey is a motif in a number of Australian fictions, including in the films, *The Road to Nhill* and *Japanese Story*.

the land

for Renate and River

I travel out across the land[1] I dream of being born in the land the land that sings my soul is flat and dry and you can see the curve of the horizon the wheat dust hits a nerve in my nose I say they're harvesting I can smell it but trained to alpine meadow grass you cannot

we sing and play games with our voices as we drive into unknown places drive off the map of the known world[2] into worlds we create for ourselves

in the back seat is the kelpie[3] brown as the land alert as a dingo some call her a red cloud kelpie fast as the wind the red dust flying

three hundred kilometres down the road we reach a town where we will refuel the car and ourselves the supermarket is a great tin shed its shelves filled with goods from baked beans and tinned tuna to T-shirts and fly nets

Olga[4] and I head for the local pool swim shower and head back out bush to camp amid ancient rocks intricately carved by time ochred by hands that have been here well before us with our modern accoutrements we have been

5 *the red Toyota*. Four-wheel drives, utilities, pick-up trucks, jeeps are the mainstay of long-distance driving holidays. Git Thadani says of herself that she has been diving her jeep around India for fifteen years. See Giti Thadani. 2004. *Moebius Trip*.

6 *Callitris*. Black cypress pine native to Australia.

known to drive nine hundred kilometres in a day we have been known to sit all day in the shade of a single tree

we break down in the strangest of places a dirt road five hours from the nearest town but it's New Year's Eve and we have packed for every eventuality two weeks of food forty litres of water and a bottle of French champagne we have run out of spare tyres and settle down to wait for help from Birdsville

the nights are rattled by storms rain pelting down on the roof of the red Toyota[5] our feet on the tailgate in the rain lightning forks the sky the kelpie shivers and curls foetal I return to the land I grew into Callitris[6] soft-needles the earth it is in my nose again the smell of freedom

there are days when the road potholes us sends us dodging boulders turns my shoulder muscles to rock the day ends with a sky filled to the brim with stars the seven sisters in flight the planets staring flatly at us the milky way that great serpentine expanse spiralling through the multiverse

these are wild days days that come and go that return us to ourselves once we shared a camp site with a kangaroo she grazed and looked at us like a spirit kangaroo mourning her loss

7 *something older*. Thadani in *Moebius Trip* (2004) explores the archaeology and etymology of lesbians in ancient India, and the destruction of these sites in recent years.

8 *deserts that are red yellow mauve*. See Nicole Bossard's *Mauve Desert* (1998).

9 *some distant time*. For an interesting and very different take on evolution see Elaine Morgan. 1973. *The Descent of Woman*.

we are not the only lesbians in a four-wheel drive around the world we go in search of something greater than ourselves something older[7] than our individual lives we scour the patterns engraved into ancient rocks the positioning of temples the resonance with earth we cross deserts that are red yellow mauve[8]

it takes us back to lagoons to the sea and the reef where we might have evolved in some distant time[9] where once we were like elephants or dolphins the rainforest rings around us cockatoos screech through the air with their lambda wings

1 *lover to me.* Sandy Jeffs in *Poems from the Madhouse* (2000) writes of a visitation from Mary: "I know you as intimately as a long-time lover." p.19.

2 *passion.* The English word "passion" comes from the Greek verb πασχω for suffering. Passion in the Biblical sense has a stronger association with suffering, than to its usual colloquial association with love.

3 *Timothy.* Many nuns take on the names of saints, male or female, and it sometimes results in such incongruities as are listed here. It's not unusual to encounter lesbians with names such as Bobby, Billy or DJ.

4 *cunning.* The word "cunning" is related to the Scots ken, to know. This is the same root from which the word "cunt" derives. There is a wonderful idiosyncratic word "cunctipotent" which means to be powerful. The power of cuncti- has been read as different from the power of omni- by some writers including Jane Caputi 2004. "Cuntspeak: Words from the heart of darkness." pp. 362-385. I use the word cunctipotence in my novel, *The Falling Woman*, 1992. p. 269. Although not etymologically defensible, cuntipotent has been taken to mean powerful in a cuntish sort of way, in other words a woman with power. The derogation which has occurred with the four letter use of the word "cunt" is perhaps an indicator of the level of woman hatred. See Beryl Fletcher. 2002. *The Word Burners*, p. 219-30.

5 *hands.* When sexual contact is forbidden any part of the body can become deeply eroticised. Touching hand-to-hand can be sexually charged.

6 *prayer wheels.* Prayer wheels are used by Buddhist nuns throughout the Himalayas. The Himalayas have a long history of association with women, indicated in part by the original name of the highest mountain in the world, Chomo-Lung Ma, which means Goddess Mother of the Universe.

angel tongues

Hail Mary Mother of God Queen of Heaven Star of the Sea you are a lover to me[1]

our bodies shiver in the cold each shiver a sacrament proof of purity our passion[2] is a cross we bear some seek solace in particular friendships Sister Timothy[3] Sister Ignatia Sister Mathias Sister Sebastian grant this day we fall into no sin

we are daughters of Babylon some of us have been whores we have sinned my left hand is cunning[4] my tongue more so have mercy upon us miserable sinners

at night in our single beds lying on tight starched sheets we have sex we are catholic girls our hands reach across to the next bed we touch our fingers sing with desire fingers follow fingers down to the webbing across the palm knuckles nails in the dark we have sex with our hands[5] our senses escaping God's custody

we pray the rosary slipping through our fingers our fingers are nimble and quick our tongues flick through the prayers collects meditations psalms chants some of us old women knead ivory beads and spin prayer wheels[6] in mountains which reach almost to heaven we intone om

7 *surly as any city gurl.* See Susan Hampton. 1989. *Surly Girls.*

8 *Beguinages.* Beguinages were all-women religious establishments of the Middle Ages. The Beguines were a Medieval grass-roots movement. They "…promised chastity during their life in the beguinage but maintained their rights to private property and worked to support themselves." Margaret Wade Labarge. 1987. *Women in Medieval Life*, p. 115. Like most good ideas of the Medieval period, in 1311 they were declared heretical by Pope Clement V. Mechtild of Magdeburg was one of the most famous mystic beguines, as famous in her time as Hildegard of Bingen. But Marguerite de Porete from Hainault suffered as many more were to in later centuries. She was accused of heresy and burnt in Paris in 1310. The Beguinage in Amsterdam is now a tourist attraction.

9 *charity.* For a lesbian reading of "charity" see Suniti Namjoshi's *Building Babel*, (1996).

10 *popes.* The only known woman pope is Pope Joan (in 854 or 855 AD Joan became Pope), and her discovery came about because she gave birth to a child while in a procession (one wonders why it took until the time of the birth to notice!). A lesbian pope prior to Pope Joan may have existed but would not have been discovered. Since Pope Joan's time every Pope has undergone a compulsory testicle test, in which the proposed incumbent is seated on a hollow chair and a committee of cardinals checks that the genitalia is of the right sex. It is then announced, *Testiculos habet et bene pendentes*, "he has testicles and they hang all right." See Barbara Walker. 1983. *The Woman's Encyclopedia of Myths and Secrets*. pp. 475-478. In 1997 Melbourne's Women's Circus dramatised the story of Pope Joan with performers wearing habits for much of the show. Pope Joan herself was portrayed as a tall stilt walker in long papal robes. See also Emily Hope. 1983. *The Legend of Pope Joan.*

11 *refectory.* The dining room of religious houses and other institutions such as prisons. The Australian radical feminist magazine *Refractory Girls* is a play on the words "refectory girls, refractory girls".

12 *winged woman.* This image comes from Revelations. There have been many dangerous winged women throughout history; they have been called unnatural. Among them are the harpies of ancient Greece, the dakinis of India, the Valkyries of Norse legend. They are represented variously as swans, ravens, crows, hawks, and in Egypt, the Middle East and India as vultures. They are probably an ancient memory of the widespread bird goddess, and are most frequently associated with death rituals. Angels could be considered a tamed Christian version of the same tradition. "The Chinese said women knew the secret of flying before men." Barbara Walker. *The Woman's Encyclopedia of Myths and Secrets*, p. 101.

13 *Babylon is fallen is fallen.* Revelations 14:8. Babylon is used over and over in the Bible as the archetypal evil city. It is filled with pagans, heathens, idolaters, adulterers, whores, buggers and no doubt, lesbians. Lesbians, like other daughters of Babylon, are fallen women. Anything reeking of women's sexuality is regarded as blasphemous in Biblical, and later Church texts.

mani padme aum clouds wrap themselves around us the peaks as sharp as a knife edge keen as a blade surly as any city gurl[7] we live in hermitages painted red wolves snow leopards prowl when food is scarce we live among women the days of our lives spent in Beguinages[8] in convents in monasteries in abbeys in nunneries in houses of caritas we are sisters of mercy we are sisters of charity[9] we are sisters to one another

some of us have become priests ministers rabbis celebrants mystics spiritual leaders and founders of religions it is harder to know whether we have ever been popes[10]

we also run laugh dance sing we eat in the refectory[11] some of us have taken a vow of silence some of us persecute ourselves with flagellation hairshirts knives cords to show our passion some have seen visions a winged woman[12] in scarlet and purple the mother of harlots of lesbians of loose women of carnal lust a friend of the lion the dragon the eagle but not of the lamb

we are fallen Babylon is fallen is fallen[13] is fallen we anoint our bodies with oil we anoint our heads with oil

there are some who work with the sick and the poor they come for refuge bruised or their bodies covered in vile

14 *the martyrs the saints the angels.* In the Church of the Death of the Madonna at Nedvigovka in Russia near the Black Sea the young woman from Rostov who was commissioned to restore the frescoes "felt that Russian Orthodox androcentrism was due for revision. The Madonna's family is entirely female, the congregation of martyrs is composed exclusively of women, the angels leaning down from the cupola to stare and laugh are all girls with Russian faces." Neal Ascherson. 1996. *Black Sea: The Birthplace of Civilisation and Barbarism*, p. 107. Valerie Solanas in the late 60s recommended that right-minded women fuck up the system. The unknown woman from Rostov seems to have done this without any assistance from her American sisters.

pustules vile bodies unclean bodies some have been infected with the plague the roses cover their bodies the children pass the walls each day singing taunting challenging God with their innocent rhymes

we work in the scriptorium with quills and brushes writing painting illuminating our fingers caress the vellum our hands decorate the words with great flourishes of colour with scarlet with gold with cerulean blue

in orthodox shrines to the Madonna we repaint the frescoes the martyrs the saints the angels[14] as a throng of women in choral ecstacy

1 *tragedy*. The word "tragedy" is derived from the Greek "η τραγη: a goat's skin; τραγικη: of or for a goat; II of or for a tragedy, tragic". Liddell and Scott. 1986. *Greek-English Lexicon*.

2 *kanji for woman*. The Japanese pictograph for woman represents a demure woman with hands folded on her knees.

3 *limbo*. When Wittig in *Across the Acheron* sets out on her journey through limbo to paradise with Manastabal, her guide, she does not know where the journey will lead nor how long it will take.

4 *Penthesileia* (Πενθεσιλεια). came to the aid of the Trojans after their local hero, Hector, son of King Priam, was killed. Penthesileia killed many Greek warriors until Achilles was persuaded to rejoin the fray, he then slew Penthesileia. For a lesbian reading of this story see Finola Moorhead. 2001. *Darkness More Visible*. In this telling Achilles is no hero, but rather a villain who does not respect the rules of war as he avenges his loss of Patroclus by raping Penthesileia.

5 *Hippolyta* ('Ιππολυτα). Associated in Athenian legend with Theseus. Some sources indicate that she was one of the Amazons to attack Athens, the war commemorated on the amazonomachy (the frieze of the Amazon's attack) still visible at the Parthenon. In other stories Theseus led or participated in an expedition against the Amazons and won Hippolyta the Queen. He then took her back with him to Athens and married her, whereupon the Amazons attacked to rescue their queen.

6 *names*. The Greek word hippos (ειπποσ) means horse. Both Lysippe (Λυσιππη) and Hippolyta ('Ιππολυτα) probably come from the same root. luo (λυω), the verb which means to loosen, to make free has verbal parts accommodating both the s and the t. λυσ- is a common prefix, while luto is a third person singular part of the verb. Alternatively, the luss- prefix could come from the word for rage or fury. In any event, both names imply wild horses, whether the wild be taken to mean free or angry. Melanippe (Μελανιππη) means black mare, while Alcippe (Αλκιππη) means powerful mare.

tragedia

they say it is a tragedy[1] when one is a lesbian but I say it is something to celebrate the lesbian has the whole world at her feet she can whistle or fly dance or climb just as her forebears her ancestors of desire have done

the emotional power of love pulls some from the safety of their fireplaces to the wilder zones of the heart where the horses gallop in the practice of freedom where the kanji for woman[2] is not demure where the word 'restriction' is an internal word

but that too they say is a tragedy to be an outsider to have a life of fear a life where the unknown rules where unpredictability leads you not by the hand but releases you insists you walk on across the mapless terrain through limbo[3] in the shadow of ravines that peak skyward

is it a tragedy to do the work you crave? is it a tragedy to spend your life in the arms of the one you love?

they tell stories of us without realising it they tell us of amazons of Penthesileia[4] Lysippe Melanippe Alcippe Hippolyta[5] great horsewomen as you can tell from their names[6] leaders in the ways of women

7 *led armies*. Penthesileia, Boudicca, St Joan all come immediately to mind. These women, amazons, and military leaders have been lesbian heroes from time to time and the subject of iconic imagery.

8 *leadership of nations*. Catherine the Great is perhaps one of the most famous of leading lesbians. Only four names are listed in *Lavender Lists*: Queen Christina of Sweden, 1632-1654, Queen Anne of England, 1702-1714, Empress Anna Ioannovna of Russia, 1730-1786, and Empress Catherine II (The Great) of Russia, 1762-1796. Lynne Yamaguchi Fletcher and Adrien Saks (Eds.). 1990. *Lavender Lists*, p. 95. Queen Christina of Sweden abdicated in order to be able to continue her relationship with Ebba Sparre. Permission not to marry meant giving up her throne. For more on this see Lillian Fardermann. 1981. *Surpassing the Love of Men*, p. 55.

9 *brought down monarchies feeding revolution*. "Among the political pamphlets which helped ignite the French Revolution is a whole group of accusations focusing on Marie Antionette's supposed tribadism and her aggressive sexuality." Lillian Faderman. 1981, *Surpassing the Love of Men*, p. 42.

10 *barbarians*. The word "barbarian" (Gr. barbaros, βαρβαροσ) means foreign, other. Lesbians, by definition in a straight world, are barbaric and behave in barbarous ways. In earlier times most of the barbarians encountered by the Greek world were from the East, some of them with long traditions of worship of female forms and goddesses, some of them amazons. It's not hard to see why lesbians are not readily elected to office.

11 *sexuality to be ignored*. "Queensland's Family First Senate candidate John Lewis said Liberal candidate for Brisbane Ingrid Tall was not getting his party's preferences because she was a lesbian." "Family First won't preference lesbians". *Sydney Morning Herald*. 5 October 2004.

12 *disproportion to our numbers*. "If all Lesbians suddenly turned purple today, society would be surprised at the number of purple people in high places." Sidney Abbot and Barbara Love. 1978. *Sappho was a Right-on Woman*.

13 *Erinna*. Erinna is linked with Sappho and best known for "a long poem written in hexameters (the meter of Homer), lamenting her childhood friend Baucis, who died soon after marriage." Margaret Williamson. 1995. *Sappho's Immortal Daughters*. p. 17. Erinna's work is described by an anonymous poet as a "Lesbian honeycomb", ibid. p. 18.

14 *Nossis*. It is possible that Nossis was descended from a line of women poets. Williamson also suggests that the references Nossis makes to roses are both allusive of desire and evocative of Sappho, "whose poems are referred to as roses", ibid. p. 19.

15 *Dickinson*. Emily Dickinson's poems are known for their cryptic and enigmatic qualities. In the last decade or so, scholars have been more willing to write about her long relationship with Susan Gilbert. It was not so easy at the time of her death and much of her correspondence was burned by members of her family to protect her privacy, or was it their reputation? See Ellen Louise Hart and Martha Nell Smith (Eds.). 1998. *Open Me Carefully: Emily Dickinson's Intimate Letters to Susan Huntington Dickinson*.

16 *Mew*. Charlotte Mew burned most of her work before killing herself. Scholars suggest that she was attempting to mask her lesbianism. Her work has re-emerged, however, precisely because of her status as a lesbian, and it has been recently published in the *Penguin Anthology of Lesbian Short Stories*. Margaret Reynolds (Ed.). 1993. *Penguin Anthology of Lesbian Short Stories*.

social mores shift and run their course we have led armies[7] commanded the navy have held the leadership of nations[8] in our hands brought down monarchies feeding revolution[9] but elected office is as rare as hen's teeth in our own countries we are barbarians[10] held in fear and loathing our constituency never large enough for our sexuality to be ignored[11]

our names come up on historical registers in disproportion to our numbers[12] the poets tell us of themselves Psappha Erinna[13] Nossis[14] Dickinson[15] Mew[16]

17 *H.D.* The original Imagist, Hilda Doolittle is a poet's poet. Her work is steeped in Greek mythology and its influence continues today. The 1980s saw a veritable H.D. industry grow around her work. There are several fine books on her life and work, but none more fascinating than *Paint It Today* the *roman à clef* which she wrote about her relationships with Francis Gregg and Bryher (Winifred Ellerman). H.D. 1992. *Paint It Today*. For biographical and literary treatments of H.D.'s life that acknowledge her as a lesbian, see Rachel Blau DuPlessis. 1986. *H.D.: The Career of That Struggle*; Susan Stanford Friedman. 1990. *Persephone's Web: Gender, Modernity, H.D.'s Fiction*. For an interesting examination of modernist lesbian writers see Gillian Hanscombe and Virgina P.M. Smyers. 1987. *Writing for Their Lives* and Jane McIntosh Snyder. 1997. *Lesbian Desire in the Lyrics of Sappho*, especially the Epilogue in which she discusses the work of H.D. and Olga Broumas.

18 *classicists*. Among the greats in this field is Jane Ellen Harrison (1850-1928), a Cambridge scholar and hugely influential in the interpretation of mythology, art and ritual. Her two most important works are *Prolegomena to the Study of Greek Religion* (1903) and *Themis: A Study of the Social Origins of Greek Religion* (1912). By the time I came to study Ancient Greek in the early 1980s, these books were out of favour, but I was able to read the copies still standing in the library stacks and not borrowed for years. They were an eye opener, and contributed enormously to my study of the language. Having the language to understand her work made it possible to plough through the war-mongering Thucydides. Virginia Woolf makes a reference to Jane Harrison in *A Room of One's Own*. For more on her life see, Sandra J. Peacock. 1988. *Jane Ellen Harrison: The Mask and the Self.* Jane's twenty-year friendship with Hope Mirlees is cast as non-sexual by Sandra Peacock but I would argue that the evidence suggests otherwise. Another classicist is "Michael Field", also poet and philosopher. She was in fact two women, Katharine Bradley (1846-1914) and Edith Cooper (1862-1913). This aunt and niece duo, also lovers, collaborated on some of the most passionate lesbian poems of the nineteenth century. See Alison Hennegan's *The Lesbian Pillow Book* (2000) and Lillian Faderman's *Surpassing the Love of Men* (1981), pp. 209-13.

19 *Greek.* Virginia Woolf lamented this in her essay "On not knowing Greek" (1968) pp. 39-59. I suspect it was also because it kept her out of the conversations of her Cambridge-educated brother, Thoby and his friends, all of whom were later to be known as the Bloomsbury Group. Barbara Deming, writing of her travels in Greece in the early 1950s, describes an epiphany at Eleusis in which the stone breasts of a statue become the possibility for claiming her self. She writes. "I am. And I will not be robbed of my sex. And I will not be shamed." Barbara Deming. 1985. *A Humming Under My Feet: A Book of Travail*, p. 221.

20 *there's no word in our language to describe what we are*. This is what Sita says to Rada in Deepa Mehta's film, *Fire*. In the face of Giti Thadani's research it appears this is not the case, although it might be true that because of hatred few wish to use the available words.

HD[17] even though their words burned flaming passions
there has never been a shortage of classicists[18] among us

many of us speak Greek[19] others among us lament that we
do not so many times I've heard them say there's no word
in our language to describe what we are[20]

we go on long journeys to ancient lands we wander
through cities cut into stone rocks hanging over us like
gardens the shapes suggestive of an entirely other world

21 *cities in our minds*. The art of memory, an art required by those interested in pursuing lesbian history and culture, involves creating a mental space, a place through which the mind can saunter at will, noticing elements of the place and its people. So long as these elements and people are tagged as memory joggers, the city in the mind can provide the possibility of speaking at length without notes, other than those places through which one is walking. See Frances Yates. 2001. *The Art of Memory*.

22 *women can hold to*. Christine de Pizan's *Book of the City of Ladies* and her *Medieval Woman's Mirror of Honour* both outline the ways in which a woman can live profitably in a city. It takes women's experience as central, and builds codes of conduct and laws upon this experience. She does not pretend that life will be easy, instead she prepares women for the inevitable adversity with which they will be confronted. In 1905 Bengal, Rokeya Hossian pondered these same questions and explored them in her story "Sultana's Dream". See Rokeya Sakhawat Hossian. 1988. *Sultana's Dream and Selections from The Secluded Ones*.

23 *our bodies giving shape to brick and stone*. The above works of imagination can be set against the archaeological records as described by Giti Thadani in her travels around India to discover ancient lesbian archaeologies. Giti Thadani. 2004. *Moebius Trip*. Two fine ancient examples of buildings which reflect the shapes of women's bodies are the Temple of Tarxien on the island of Malta and Skara Brae in Scotland. The shapes of these and other tombs and dwellings are shown in Cristina Biaggi. 1994. *Habitations of the Great Goddess*. p. 127. For a lesbian story centred on Skara Brae see Cathie Dunsford 2001. *Song of the Selkies*.

24 *rooms burrowed into the earth*. The Hypogeum of the Temple of Hal Saflieni in Malta, is the largest of all underground buildings, encompassing 600 square metres and extending more than 10 metres into the earth. The Hypogeum consists of one or more egg shaped chambers situated underground. Cristina Biaggi. 1994. *Habitations of the Great Goddess*. p. 29. A fictional rendering of such underground dwellings appears in Sally Gearheart's utopian novel, *The Wanderground*. She creates the Remembering Rooms which are fashioned to resemble the cochlea of the inner ear (they are called the Kochlias). Sally Gearheart. 1979. *The Wanderground*. This novel was very influential for many lesbians in the late 1970s and early 1980s. Remembering is an act of resistance for lesbians, for without active remembering we can forget or not recognise even the lovers we have had. See Andrea Dworkin's short story "The simple story of a lesbian girlhood" in *The New Woman's Broken Heart* (1980).

25 *rent by strife*. Monique Wittig's San Francisco, as depicted in *Across the Acheron*, is deeply divided, and the divisions include the fights and arguments of lesbians who hold to different politics. Similarly, the zappers in *Building Babel* show the divisions in the city of Babel. They possess shiny steel claws of varying voltage; the higher the voltage, the higher the social position or closeness to Queen Alice. Suniti Namjoshi. 1996. *Building Babel*, pp. 129-131.

26 *unscrupulous women*. Queen Alice in *Building Babel* is one such character. She has determined to be a dictator and insists on total loyalty from her followers. Reminiscent of the Red Queen, she is quick to order, "Off with their heads." Suniti Namjoshi. 1996. *Building Babel*, pp. 104-140.

27 *not even lesbians*. An ironic statement to say the least. Lesbians, of course, are as frail as any other group of people. Our dispossessed status sometimes confers an advantage of insight, for some it simply continues the violence of our lives. One can celebrate a culture, such as lesbian culture, without holding to the proposition that all its members are wonderful individuals. Gillian Hanscombe explores the idea of evil in lesbian feminists in her novel. Gillian Hanscombe. 1995. *Figments of a Murder*.

there are cities in our minds[21] some we have invented cities built solely for women cities inhabited by women cities with rules which women can hold to[22] the architecture based on the bodies of women our bodies giving shape to brick and stone[23]

some are underground cities rooms burrowed into the earth[24] some of these cities are rent by strife[25] and argument or are ruled by unscrupulous women[26] we're not perfect I say not even lesbians[27]

28 *cyborgs*. Pauline Hanson, a controversial Australian right-wing politician, was reported to have said that in a few decades time Australia would be led by a "lesbian cyborg". This is reported by Babette Francis in The Joint Standing Committee on Treaties, Melbourne, 10 July 1997. Canberra: Commonwealth of Australia, Hansard. TR1005, p. 61.

29 *damned women*. The translation usually given for Baudelaire's two poems entitled Les Femmes Damnées is "Lesbians". See Marthiel and Jackson Mathews (Eds.). 1989. *Charles Baudelaire: The Flowers of Evil*. Poems CXV and CXVI. Monique Wittig alludes to Baudelaire also in *Across the Acheron* where she uses the terms "condemned souls" (p. 8) and "damned souls" (p. 36). Wittig rarely fails to use words to good purpose.

30 *corrupts the family*. In 2004 just before the Australian federal election a Family First campaign worker answered "'yes' to a question about whether Family First supported lesbians being burned to death." *Sydney Morning Herald*. 5 October 2004. For a fictional response to this see Susan Hawthorne. 2004b. "A Family Fable", *Hecate*, pp. 127-8; and *Rain and Thunder*. Issue 25, p. 33.

31 *tortured*. There is very little research on the torture of lesbians. The best personal account I have located is Consuelo Rivera-Fuentes and Lynda Burke. 2001. "Talking With/In Pain: Reflections on bodies under torture." pp. 653-668. See also my article "Research and Silence" (2004a).

32 *out of existence*. Evelyn Torton Beck writes "According to Jewish Law, this book is written by people who do not exist. I assure you, it's all very logical: we're not proscribed because we don't exist. If we existed, believe me, they'd be against us." Evelyn Torton Beck. (Ed.). 1982. *Nice Jewish Girls*, p. xiii. Queen Victoria also apparently did not believe in the existence of lesbians; and the Chinese authorities after the Communist revolution declared that there were no lesbians and no flies in China. Strangely, in spite of this, lesbians have been persecuted by the state and the church. Nazis found lesbians, as did the witch burners of the "Renaissance" period.

33 *Lesbian Linear B*. In a series of hand-made porcelain books, Suzanne Bellamy plays with the possibilities of a lesbian library which she entitles The Little Lesbian Book Series. Among the titles of this series is *Lesbian Linear B*. Other titles include *City of Lesbians*, *New Lesbian Foreign Policy*, *The Lesbian Fractal* and *Pruning the Lesbian Rose*. Only one copy of each title is fired.

34 *Linear A*. Dorothy Porter uses the metaphor of Linear A, an undeciphered script to date, to describe the unknown emotional forces of discovering one's sexuality at twenty-two. Dorothy Porter. 1996. "Linear A." *Crete*, p 6.

35 *loss of memory*. For a theoretical discussion of this see Susan Hawthorne. 2003. "The Depoliticising of Lesbian Culture." *Hecate*. Also see VS. 1999. *Facing the Mirror*, pp. 147-8. Giti Thadani. 1996. *Sakhiyani*, pp. 1-8.

36 *suicide*. An interesting analysis of suicide is provided in Giti Thadani. 1996. *Sakhiyani*, pp. 101-104.

those who fear us have many names for their fear we are as frightening as wild animals as unknown as cyborgs[28] we are damned women[29] our very existence poisons the young corrupts the family[30]

we have been ostracised excommunicated tortured[31] fired expelled killed named out of existence[32]

we thrill at the prospect of reading Sappho in her own tongue of discovering our own Lesbian Linear B[33] or Linear A[34] in the spiral hieroglyphs we grasp at the fragments of our culture shining like mythic jewels

the tragedy of lesbian existence is the loss of memory[35] the repetitions of fictions of unrequited love of passion for a thing that melts away in fear we pull out our hair in grief go mad commit suicide[36] we are pitied for our sunken

37 *wolves*. Olga Broumas in her poem, "Little Red Riding Hood" writes that she is waiting, across this improbable forest / peopled with wolves and our lost, flower-gathering /sisters they feed on. Olga Broumas. 1977. *Beginning with O*. p. 68. The sisters are at once flower-gatherers and wolves; at once sexually expressive and the subject of sexual expression.

Another improbable forest appears in Suniti Namjoshi's fable "Wolf", which tells the tale of a friendship which develops between a virgin and a wolf. The hunters are immediately suspicious that the virgin is using the wolf to guard her virginity (although Namjoshi explains that they just happened to get on and became friends). Knowing best, although they were never able to slay the wolf or find the wolf's friend, the virgin, the hunters: "decided the forest had swallowed them, so they put up a sign on the edge of their town in large red letters warning the unwary that there were wolves around." Suniti Namjoshi. 1993. *St Suniti and the Dragon*, p. 86.

That this is equivalent to putting up a neon sign with the message "Beware: Lesbians in this Area" is confirmed by the story which follows "Wolf". "Subsequent History" has the wolf and the virgin walking on through several villages, being rejected or accepted only on impossible conditions (pulling out the wolf's claws and teeth – read: her frightening sexuality; the virgin marrying someone – read: taming and occupying her sexuality). And so they walk on: "until, at last, they entered a realm that is not as yet familiar to us." Namjoshi, *St Suniti and the Dragon*. p. 87.

38 *Her*. See H.D. 1981. *HERmione*. The HER of this novel is Frances Gregg

39 *goat*. Latin, caper, capri. Capri: The island of goats. A favourite hangout for lesbians of the 1920s. Also the brand name of a sportscar, driven by the lesbian with a penchant for the wind in her hair.

40 *write slant*. Writing slant was what Emily Dickinson advised in Poem 1129 which begins "Tell all the Truth but tell it slant–". See *The Complete Poems of Emily Dickinson*. (1960).

41 *why is the measure of love lost*. Jeanette Winterson. 1993. *Written on the Body*. p. 1.

sleepless eyes reviled for our appetites we are poor sisters our souls condemned to wander through forests and deserts like hungry wolves[37]

some of us cannot speak our pain or we sob as we confess undying love for Her[38] in ancient times we sacrificed a goat[39] the creature who can climb mountains backwards picking at leaves as it goes the goat whose death signals our release into the drama of life the script we can rewrite write slant[40] if we will they replay these scripts in an effort to make us believe them

I ask why is the measure of love loss?[41]

1 *"write, write or die"*. H.D. 1972. *Hermetic Definition*, p. 7.

2 *adorn walls*. The contemporary version of this is graffiti, whether it be found on public walls or the more intimate walls of women's toilets.

3 *terracotta pots*. The oldest fragment of poetry by Sappho is found on a piece of broken terracotta pottery. It is a copy of a Sappho poem and dates from the third or second century BCE. Margaret Williamson argues that because of the large number of errors in the copy, it may have been copied for use in a classroom. The poem, "Prayer for Aphrodite's Presence" (Fragment 2) contains these lines: " therein cold water babbles through apple-branches, and the whole place is shadowed by roses, and from the shimmering leaves the sleep of enchantment comes down". Margaret Williamson. 1995. *Sappho's Immortal Daughters*, pp. 57-58.

4 *pillowslips*. Gertrude Stein's "a rose is a rose is a rose" is said to have been embroidered around a circlet of roses on a linen pillowslip. Alison Hennegan called her anthology of lesbian writings, *The Lesbian Pillow Book* (2000) a reference to *The Pillow Book of Sei Shonagon*. Sei Shonagon may not have been a lesbian, but her work has inspired many women readers over the last millennium and several lesbian pillow books have been published which suggests that lesbians rarely rise from our beds!

5 *burnt*. Sappho's poetry was burnt in great quantities by the Church Fathers. As a symbolic gesture towards the loss of so much of her poetry Monique Wittig and Sande Zeig, in a page devoted to her in *Lesbian Peoples*, put Sappho's name at the top of a blank page. Reading the work of Sappho involves reading between the lines, imagining what words might lie around the fragments. It is a fitting metaphor for the history of lesbians, where so much is not known, has not been recorded, or has been deliberately destroyed, that the researcher becomes a scholarly detective. Monique Wittig and Sande Zeig. 1979. *Lesbian Peoples*, p. 136.

6 *love itself is an uprising*. Love between women has certainly caused uprisings. In early December 1998 movie theatres in Bombay and other Indian cities were attacked by rioting crowds in order to force the closure of cinemas showing Deepa Mehta's controversial film, *Fire*, which culminates in a lesbian love scene. One of those supporting the rioters, Pramod Nayalkar, State Culture Minister for Maharashtra, was fearful that the film could destroy Indian culture. He said, "If women's physical needs get fulfilled through lesbian acts, the institution of marriage will collapse, reproduction of human beings will stop." Ian Mackinnon. 1998. "Film's followers fight fire with fire." *The Australian*, p. 9.

7 *bring down governments*. During the French Revolution, which declared brotherhood a freedom, Marie Antoinette was the subject of pamphlets attacking her sexuality and in particular "tribadism" or lesbian sexual practices. Faderman argues that the pamphlets displayed hostility towards the Queen's power. Lillian Faderman. 1981. *Surpassing the Love of Men*, p. 42.

8 *defy gravity*. A solo aerials performance of *Gravity Defied* was part of the Sydney 2002 Gay Games. Newtown New Works, New Theatre, King Street, Newtown, Sydney 4-5 November. I was the aerialist.

9 *alphabet of desire*. See "Erotica Alphabetica." In Susan Hawthorne and Jenny Pausacker (Eds.). 1989. *Moments of Desire*, p. 21.

love is an uprising

we *write write or die*[1] is our anthem our poems adorn walls[2] parchment papyri terracotta pots[3] quilts embroidery samples even pillowslips[4]

our words are burnt[5] these are not violent words unless love itself is an uprising[6] they are words of affection of particular friendships of friendships we make public by decorating our bodies with paint by encircling our bodies with garlands of flowers the ankles the wrists the waist the neck spilling with colour the flowers of these friendships barely fading

between us declarations of love can shatter families bring down governments[7] wreck the economy create civil war

all the same we declare love declare love between us

we are experimenters with language our words defy gravity[8] explore unknown shores in our isolation we believe that our experience has not been written about so we are inventive with form with words with metaphor we learn to read the alphabet of desire[9]

10 *language invented by women*. Aside from the reasonable proposition that women invented language, there are languages consciously invented by women which contain words for concepts which are almost unthinkable in English. Suzette Haden Elgin's Láadan, which she invented for her speculative fiction *Native Tongue*, is perhaps the most famous. The Dictionary includes the word *rarilh*: "to deliberately refrain from recording; for example the failure throughout history to record the accomplishments of women" [or lesbians]. Suzette Haden Elgin. 2000. *Native Tongue*, p. 303. Or, "like amnesics / in a ward on fire, we must / find words or burn." Olga Broumas. 1977. *Beginning with O*, p. 24.

11 *some of us write in it*. Nüshi or Nüshu is a written language from Hunan Province in China used only by women. For more information see Robin Morgan. 1992. "The Word of a Woman" in *The Word of a Woman: Selected Prose 1968-1992*. Interestingly, the Chinese character nú means slave, and is composed of nü (woman) and yòu (hand). Barbara Niederer.1995. *China for Women: Travel and Culture*, p. 9. The book was originally published as *China der Frauen* in German by Frauenoffensive, 1989.

12 *codes*. A fine example of this is Anne Lister, whose mid-nineteenth century diaries are slowly being decoded. They have been called the Rosetta stone of lesbian culture, and consist of millions of words. See Jill Liddington. 1998. *Female Fortune*.

13 *reproduce*. "To the question, 'How will lesbians reproduce?' asked during a large assembly, one of the Red Dykes, thus named in sheer modesty, let out quite by chance the now famous reply, 'By the ear.' Thus the little companion lovers are born today from ear to ear." Monique Wittig and Sande Zeig. 1979. *Lesbian Peoples*, p. 49. Storytelling, whispering, rumour, gossip, word of mouth have been the primary mode of passing on lesbian culture.

14 *ears*. Sally Gearheart's novel, *The Wanderground*, elaborates metaphorically on the idea of the ear as central to lesbian existence. The underground habitations of the women in this novel are called the Kochlias. Cochlea (Gr. κοχλιας) is the spiral cavity of the inner ear. It is also used to describe the spiral shape of a snail's shell. Sally Gearheart. 1979. *The Wanderground*.

15 *listening*. "In the beginning was not the word. In the beginning is the hearing." Mary Daly. 1978. *Gyn/Ecology*, p. 424.

16 *galactic*. In the whimsical "Night Cows", Jovette Marchessault depicts lesbians and female animals meeting nightly in the Milky Way. She writes: "They come on two feet and on four, the terrestrial motors of their hearts are swelling the white cantata of the milky way." Jovette Marchessault. 1985. *Lesbian Triptych*. p. 76. The word galactic is derived from the Greek gala – γαλα, meaning milk.

17 *tenth muse*. See the chapter on Sappho as the tenth muse in Margaret Reynolds. 2001. *The Sappho Companion*, pp. 67-78.

18 *solitude*. Sister Solitude, aka Solly is a character in Suniti Namjoshi. 1996. *Building Babel*.

we imagine a language invented by women[10] some of us write in it[11] or we invent our own codes[12] our metaphors and images we invent words for experiences common among us but rare in other parts of society we reproduce[13] through language heard and spoken written and sung our ears[14] listening[15] down through the ages the distances as great as galactic[16] space time measured in light years

we have an ear for music and for poetry our balance honed like a cat's our sense of touch as fine and strong as the spider's bouncing and spinning on her web

we are poets and congregate in circles listening to the inheritance of the tenth muse[17] we read and chant our work to audiences in rapt silence we part moving back into solitude[18] scribbling and tapping away until we coalesce into molecules of words

19 *saints*. Suniti Namjoshi asks, "Are poets by definition always saintly?" *St Suniti and the Dragon*, p. 35. In India poets are considered saints, this lesbian poet wonders whether they will give her the honour of sainthood, especially as she is "not a proper woman". See Suniti Namjoshi. 1993. *St Suniti and the Dragon*, p. 19. Perhaps she's a lemon.

20 *sybils*. "A lesbian, like the sybil, lives out of time, out of place, out of history. She is an aberration. Her social identity is factitious – a grotesquerie somehow accommodated at dinner parties, at weddings and funerals, in workplaces, on census forms. I claim the sybil because there are thousands of us who also want to tell the truth: to each other and to anyone." See Gillian Hanscombe. 1992. *Sybil: The Glide of her Tongue*, p. xiv.

21 *Cassandras*. Cassandra's ears were licked by serpents when she was a child and, as a result, she was able to hear the future. She prophesied the fall of Troy but was doomed never to be believed. This has also been the fate of many lesbians. "We talk of Cassandra. Belief is as important as knowledge. For what is knowledge if no one believes it? There have been many times when destruction could have been avoided, when the future was glaring at people. That was the fate of Cassandra, though her ears had been licked by a serpent, no one would believe her prophesies. //They laughed at her story of the wooden horse – and the city fell. They laughed even as they died. //There have been many Cassandras. Many of us." Susan Hawthorne. 1992. *The Falling Woman*, p. 86

some of us are saints[19] or Sybils[20] or Cassandras[21] some are convinced that the world needs to hear our words others are demure or loud

whatever kind of poet we may be each is convinced of her worth of her need to write write or die

1 *between.* Metaxu (Gr. μεταξυ) describes the between force. The metaxu is anything which allows two entities to join. It is connectivity. It is the state between two worlds, two times. It is the world of amphibians, creatures able to live in two mediums. Lesbians live in at least two worlds, and can therefore be said to inhabit the metaxu, the twilight zone, the lavender hour.

2 *lemon-scented.* See Lisa Bellear's poem "Chops 'n' Things" in *Dreaming in Urban Areas* (1996).

3 *asocials.* Under the Nazi regime "asocials" was a very flexible label which included prostitutes, criminals, the homeless, unemployed, Gypsies – including Roma and Sinti – as well as lesbians. Claudia Schoppmann. 1996. *Days of Masquerade: Life stories of lesbians during the Third Reich*, p. 21.

4 *she did not make it through the war.* For information on the fate of lesbians under Nazism see Moniker Reinfelder 1996. "Persecution and Resistance". In Monika Reinfelder (Ed.). *Amazon to Zami*, pp. 11-29. For a very personal account see Erica Fischer. 1994. *Aimée and Jaguar*.

lavender hour

in the lavender hour between[1] winter afternoon tea and dusk my lover and I stroll the streets hand in hand we walk beneath lemon-scented[2] gums our noses twitching

in the lavender hour lives are changed forever

in Shanghai we waltz on the Bund at dawn our bodies moving to the rhythm we learnt a generation ago held in the memory of our muscles we used to drink in the bars listen to jazz and kiss in the corners no one noticed us for fifty years they said we did not exist now we teach the young ones the secrets of the waltz and of old Shanghai

in the lavender hour we have walked toward gas chambers along with gypsies Jews prostitutes those proclaimed mentally or physically defective asocials[3] all of us

I'm a Hungarian gypsy Jew she said one day as we walked through the Botanic Gardens past the black swans craning their necks and waddling ungracefully toward the scrap of bread my father escaped from three death marches my aunt was not so lucky a gypsy a Jew and a lesbian she did not make it through the war[4]

5 *Uranian*. The term Uranianism was used in the early twentieth century as a term for lesbianism. Elizabeth Dauthendey. 1906. *The Uranian Question and Women*.

6 *you're not safe here*. She was referring to the records of the torture of lesbians under the socialist government of Yoweri Museveni. See Amnesty International. 2001. *Crimes of hate, conspiracy of silence, Torture and ill-treatment based on sexual identity* ACT 40/016/2001.

7 *goblin markets*. The goblin markets about which Christina Rosetti writes take place during twilight. Two sisters living on the edge of fairyland are forbidden social intercourse with the fruit peddling goblins. One sister, Laura, gives in, and rather like Snow White, Eve and Sappho before her, eats the fruit. So begins a process of inward wasting, until her sister Lizzie prepares to sacrifice herself by going into the twilight and obtaining a second taste of the fruit. Laura's health is restored. For a critical examination of the poem, see Jan Marsh. 1994. *Christina Rosetti: A Literary Biography*, pp. 229-237.

8 *hussies*. An Adelaide-based lesbian band of the 1970s called itself the Shameless Hussies. A band member, Helen Potter, wrote the eponymous song which has the chorus: "We're shameless hussies and we don't give a damn / we're loud and raucous and we're fighting for our rights / and our sex and for fun, and we're strong." The song travelled around Australia and in the 1980s was taken to Greenham Common where it was reproduced in the *Greenham Common Song Book*.

9 *circus freaks*. Bearded women, aka lesbians, have earned their keep as freaks in circuses up to the middle of the twentieth century. If no women in western society ever plucked, shaved, waxed, exfoliated or laser beamed their facial hair there would be many more bearded women in the streets.

10 *fingers*. "Then dawn's / pink fingers / could infiltrate your body." Susan Hawthorne. 1997. "Dialogues with Love". In *Fruit Salad*, p. 186.

11 *virtual worlds cyberspace*. An interesting conundrum: as William Gibson has pointed out, in cyberspace there's no there there; and as so many repressive regimes have pointed out, lesbians don't exist.

12 *lesbian heavens*. Another place which doesn't yet exist, but if Dawn Cohen has her way, in Lesbian Heaven: "There are Lesbian trees / and a Lesbian breeze, / a Lesbian moon at night / Lesbian lakes and Lesbian seas / That sparkle in Lesbian light". Dawn Cohen. 1989. "Lesbian Heaven". In Susan Hawthorne and Jenny Pausacker (Eds.). 1989. *Moments of Desire*, pp. 62-63.

13 *that harbour that haven*. As H.D. writes in *Trilogy*: "*we know no rule / of procedure, // we are voyagers, discoverers / of the not known, // the unrecorded; / we have no map; // possibly we will reach haven, / heaven.*" H.D. 1983. *Collected Poems*, p. 543. Italics in the original.

in the lavender hour extraterrestrial lesbians slip between worlds our faces as frightening as that of the Gorgon if you look at me you will likely turn to stone we are captives of Venus Martian in our sexual style our origins are Uranian[5] our desires Plutonic our mood Saturnian to the point of lunacy truly we are inter-planetary

in Uganda it was Nora who said to me be careful you're not safe here[6] will I turn to stone? be accused of unearthly crimes?

at the goblin markets[7] we eat the fruit of goblins eat the seeds of the pomegranate we are not trapped in underground prisons we do not turn into a pillar of salt for no man looks at us with that gaze

we inhabit the twilight world of harpies hags and hussies[8] we are monstrous beings circus freaks[9] and out of this world

the Greeks knew that we lurked in the between spaces of dawn prying apart the veil of time with rose-tipped fingers[10]

you can find us in places which don't exist yet virtual worlds cyberspace[11] and lesbian heavens[12] we are journeying there maybe one day we'll sail into that harbour that haven[13]

14 *it's in our bones our ligaments*. For a truly in-the-body experience read Monique Wittig. 1975. *The Lesbian Body*.

15 *blood sisters*. See Valerie Miner. 1982. *Blood Sisters*. For an anthology of writings by lesbian sisters see Lee Fleming. 1995. *To Sappho, My Sister: Lesbian Sisters Write About Their Lives*.

16 *desire*. According to Jovette Marchessault, in the lesbian calendar "eveything is accomplished through desire. ... desire which prevents neutrality from taking over." Jovette Marchessault. 1985. *Lesbian Triptych*, p. 42. See also Dawn Cohen's poem "Lesbian Heaven" in Susan Hawthorne and Jenny Pausacker (Eds.). 1989. *Moments of Desire*, pp. 62-63.

the lavender hour is not marked on any clock face or measurable by digital timers it cannot be found in sidereal time for the lavender hour shifts with the days and the seasons it can happen at any time that the world rolls over and turns purple but whatever the time it will be a moment of clarity

we are moved viscerally by the redemptive power of love of desire it's in our bones our ligaments[14] our muscles and corpuscles we are sisters of the flesh skin sisters blood sisters[15]

the lavender hour is not even marked on the lesbian almanac which is equally mercurial made up as it is of moments of desire[16]

1 *Carnivale*. "Carnivale". Script for POW small show. First performed at Swinburne University, Lilydale Campus. 1 December, 1998.

2 *O*. The O has been used by lesbian writers on numerous occasions. Olga Broumas' first collection of poems (1977) is entitled *Beginning with O*. Monique Wittig uses the O as the first chapter opener (p. 3) in *The Guérillères*. These images of lacunae recur in the text on pp. 51 and 105. As a lesbian reader in the 1970s these circles seemed affirming of the decision I had made in regard to my sexuality. Gertrude Stein with her "A rose is a rose is a rose" later made it into a ring, an O, of roses. Gertrude Stein. 1935. *Lectures in America*, p. 231. Dante proposed that the original (male) name of god was i. I suggest it is O. Kay Gardner, in *Sounding the Inner Landscape* creates images of intervals. The O represents unison, singing at the same pitch. Sameness. See Kay Gardner. 1997. *Sounding the Inner Landscape*, p. 105. For a critique of David Le Vay's English translation of Wittig's *The Lesbian Body* and his use of "I" in the text, see Namascar Shaktini's "Displacing the Phallic Subject" (1982).

3 *wolf*. The wolf has been interpreted as a symbol of aggressive male sexuality, but feminist and lesbian writers have turned this idea on its head. Renée Vivien in her story, "The Woman of the Wolf", writes of a woman who would rather die with her pet wolf in the sea, than respond to the sexual advances of the man telling the story. See Renée Vivien. 1983. *The Woman of the Wolf and other stories*. Barnes uses the image of the wolf to represent repressed sexuality, the sexuality society forced lesbians to hide. The wolf, nevertheless, emerges in the dark of the night. See Djuna Barnes. 1936. *Nightwood*. Was it Djuna Barnes' wolf that inspired the irrepressible girls at Vassar? See Anne Mackay (Ed.). 1993. *Wolf Girls at Vassar*.

4 *companion lovers*. "The companion lovers gather from lesbians all of the culture, the past, the inventions, the songs and the ways of life." They are engaged in much the same project as this series of poems. See Monique Wittig and Sande Zeig. 1979 *A Dictionary of Lesbian Peoples*, p. 35.

5 *masks*. If you go to Venice look for the masks of Carnivale which are for sale in the little shops a few steps below street level.

6 *crowds*. We often meet in crowds. It is safer that way. We form crowds at street demonstrations, at dance parties and lesbian balls, when lesbian singers come to town, and when Martina Navratilova or one of her descendants is playing on the centre court at Kooyong.

7 *joglaresas*. Joglaresas were Moorish women jugglers who were part of the retinue of the Occitanian ruling class in the tenth and eleventh centuries. It was from this base that the Troubadors arose in subsequent centuries. An image of a late 10th century joglaresa can be found in the St. Martial Codex, held in the Bibliothèque Nationale, France. It also appears in Meg Bogin. 1976. *The Women Troubadors*, p. 48. Referring to this time Monique Wittig and Sande Zeig say that companion lovers began to juggle during the dark ages to cheer it up. Monique Wittig and Sande Zeig. 1979. *Lesbian Peoples*, p. 88.

8 *spin*. Spinning is a particularly female occupation, whether it be spinning yarn, spinning out a tale (a yarn), spinning and sparking in a Dalyesque manner or spinning like a spider on a web.

carnivale[1]

we sing sliding along arpeggios stringing out the sounds
the rhythm of our heartbeats in time to the music

we chant beginning with O[2] like the chorister and the lesbian the howl of the wolf[3] woman and her companion lovers[4]

we don masks[5] of black gold silver white and splashes of colour we disguise the extrovert the streets are filled with crowds[6] everyone disguised and in our new personae we explore the wilds of our emotions here are bridal pairs exchanging vows mid-canal with grappa in coloured Venetian glasses

carnivale is here the crowds could be from any time a medieval feast a painting by Bosch or Carpaccio jugglers and joglaresas[7] stand side by side the one throwing balls the other tossing notes into the cold air pigeons play shadow games

children roll hoops or spin[8] by on knife-thin blades the tarot reader spins her own stories unravelling the future from the past a Norn crouches in an archway

9 *Queen of Hearts*. In a deck of cards this is the lesbian card of love. In the Tarot she is the Queen of Cups. Jeanette Winterson goes in search of the Queen of Hearts in *The Passion* (1987). Judy Grahn has written two collections of poems focusing on the card queens, *The Queen of Wands* (1982) and *The Queen of Swords* (1987). In the preface to *The Queen of Wands* she writes that *The Queen of Cups* (or Hearts) and *The Queen of Diamonds* are to follow, p. xi.

10 *thread*. In the labyrinth, the house of the labrys, of the double axe, love is sought by means of a thread. It is not clear whether love will be a monster or a tame being; one has to enter the labyrinth to find out.

12 *unicyclists*. It matters little whether the cycle is a unicycle or a bicycle, a woman riding such a contraption must be a lesbian. Divided skirts, or bloomers, were invented so women could ride bicycles. It took some bravery to do so at the dawn of the bicycle's invention, and those women who did were soon equated with feminists / lesbians.

12 *fly without fear*. Like the cyclists, women who join a circus, take up trapeze in adulthood and who have overcome their fear of heights, if ever they had such fears, are readily seen as odd, other, or as a lesbian.

13 *standing one atop the other*. In a performance of this poem produced by Performing Older Women's Circus members, four women stood one atop the other in the balance called "tiers facing".

14 *gamelan orchestra*. Helen Pausacker, a Melbourne-based writer, first gave me an appreciation of the complexity of Balinese shadow puppets and the accompanying gamelan music. She performed in Melbourne in the 1980s at Salon-A-Muse, a venue established by a group of lesbians to encourage artistic and intellectual endeavours by women.

15 *webbed feet*. The gondoliers of Venice are said to be born with webbed feet. See Jeanette Winterson. 1987. *The Passion*.

the Queen of Hearts the Queen of Hearts[9] she follows the thread[10] into the palazzo unravels the tapestry unravels her life casting it off all for the Queen of Hearts

back in the streets the crowd moves like a symphony here come the unicyclists[11] and a caravanserai of elephants lions seals and women who fly without fear[12]

they are like some forgotten circus troupe telling tearful tales Aesop's animals standing one atop the other[13] until sunrise and the highest crows the morning's welcome

along the waterways come gondoliers as silent as shadow puppets in a gamelan orchestra[14] decked in their finery strange footwear covering webbed feet[15] the drummers

16 *webs*. In aerials, a web is a long thick rope hung from a high joint. It has a hand or foot grip from which the aerialist is suspended. She uses this as a point from which to make bodily shapes. When the rope is spun from below she can control her speed by forming a tight ball (in which case she will spin faster) or by stretching out her limbs (in which case she will slow down). The spider who weaves a web is related to women in many mythical traditions. "The Greek Arachne, the Native American Spider Woman, and tales of the Black Widow all have resonance … The word spider is derived from Old English spinnan 'to spin'." Marta Weigle. 1982. *Spiders and Spinsters: Women and Mythology.* p. 2. A webster, as Judy Grahn points out, "formerly meant 'female weaver'." Judy Grahn. 1982. *The Queen of Wands*, p. xiii; see also her comparisons of the Ainu peoples of Hokkaido, Japan with the Pueblo stories of Spider Woman, pp. 98-99. For a longer discussion of Spider Grandmother/Spider Woman see Paula Gunn Allen who writes of the centrality of Spider Grandmother in the Keres Pueblo Indians' universe. See her book, *The Sacred Hoop*. 1986.

17 *dervish*. "a spinster, a whirling dervish, spinning in a new time/space." Mary Daly. 1978. *Gyn/Ecology*, pp. 3-4.

18 *have you met your shadow head on*. The Black Piglet, in Suniti Namjoshi's *Building Babel*, meets Death. "As she nosed among the bushes and turned up stones, she saw a black shadow out of the corner of her eye. A perspicacious piglet, she realised at once that this must be Death." Suniti Namjoshi. 1996. *Building Babel*, p. 14.

join the throng beating out the heart's rhythm aerialists spin from webs[16] their bodies clump and open spiralling in a dizzying dervish[17] dance

and death too crawls by selecting victims at random is your number up? have you met your shadow head on?[18]

the dancers the celibates the poets the tree climbers the hand surgeons the teachers the sybils the artists the revellers the lovers are all here

we fling ourselves toward the finale all whistling all drumming all singing a great chorale of voices and bodies swirling swaying spinning flying

we revel until dawn when the sun rises once again over the sea mirror-like creating time spilling us into our days where we create new worlds and survive this one

April 1997–April 2005

composition

music for lesbian mouths

ooooooooooooooooooooooooooooooooooooooo

oooo OOO ooooo OO OO OO OO

O-oo oo-O

O

O O O O O

O O O

OOOOOO OOO O O

O

dialogues with death

Death,
you have an unfair advantage—
you know the rules.

almanac of the dead[1]

for Primrose McDonald Hawthorne
1 July 1924 to 3 May 1994

i

We agree to meet at a restaurant.
There are eight of us from three generations.

It is noisy and we cannot converse easily.
I can hardly hear what you say.

Each time we sit, you and I are separated.

As we walk back to the car, after ice-creams
by the river, my sister and I walk ahead.

I am aware that you are watching from behind.

An unwanted thought,
It would be terrible if this were the last time I saw you.

ii

The next day I feel uneasy.
I could have rung, but I
resisted the urge, feeling
ridiculous about my uneasiness.

I say nothing.

iii

I ring you after you are home again—
three hundred miles away.

1 Leslie Marmon Silko. 1991. *Almanac of the Dead*

iv
I begin reading *Almanac of the Dead*.

v
You do not ring me before I leave for America.
This is unusual.
In a plane over the Pacific, I think of this
and again feel the urge to ring.

It's only ten days.
Did I forget to tell you?

vi
I shop in Santa Barbara.
I buy,
one pair of black trousers
one pair of black socks
one black linen jacket.

vii
I am to read and give a paper at a conference—
you are mentioned in this paper.

viii
At eight o'clock on the morning of my paper
I get a phone call.

That is when I learn you've had a heart attack.

ix
I go to breakfast and mention this to a colleague.

If your mother is in hospital, she'll be all right.
No one dies of heart attack if they've made it to the hospital.

x
During the reading, a poet almost breaks down
reading a poem about her mother.
She tells me later that her mother is ninety
and it's beginning to worry her.

xi
At the end of the day another poet tells me
his father died when he was at a conference last year.

xii
I drive an American academic back to the hotel via the beach.
She tells me of a paper she had heard by a woman who
had arrived ten minutes after her mother died.

xiii
I am reading *Almanac of the Dead*.

xiv
I ring you at the hospital.
You get out of bed to speak to me.
You say, *This is expensive, Dear,*
I'd better go.

Wait a minute, I say,
Tell me what happened.

You tell me of the garden tour,
the pain, the ambulance
from Braidwood to Canberra.

I'll be back on the fifth, I say.
You say, *Oh …*

xv
The rest of the family say
you'll be home next weekend.

xvi
I realise that I leave on the fifth
and don't get home until the seventh.

xvii
Early the next day, I ring.
Late the next day, I ring again.

Each time I ring you are asleep.

xviii
I try to get on that night's flight,
but as I speak the plane from Santa Barbara
to LA flies over the motel.

The drive to LA is too long.
I book for the next night's flight. The first.
I cancel my five days in San Francisco.

xix
As I drive to LA I talk to you.
Tears stream down my face.
Mum, don't die before I get there.

xx
Against all odds I run into
the one person I know in LA.
This calms me.
I feel protected.

xxi
From the Melbourne airport,
I ring you.

You are asleep.

xxii
I am still reading *Almanac of the Dead*.

xxiii
I arrive at the hospital.
A nurse asks me to wait in the family room.
I assume she's gone to tell you I've arrived.

xxiv
Dad comes through the plastic doors.
You're too late, Dear.

xxv
I ask to see you.
You are sad and grey.

xxvi
Two days later I wear
the black pants,
black socks,
black jacket
to your funeral

xxvii
I have finished reading *Almanac of the Dead.*

graveside meditation

We, the mourners, stand— the
four of us in a line beside the
grave, beside the coffin.

You, my father— your face dark
and etched with lines of
disbelief— your white hair stark
in this sunny cemetery— you are
motionless— a grid of grief.

In the row behind stands our
aunt— our mother's friend for
more than sixty years

—she, the aunt— leans forward
and passes to you my sister—
seven roses picked from her
rambling garden

—she passes the roses to you—
some pink, some primrose, some
that lovely mix of pink and
yellow

—she passes them and you step
forward and place them on the
coffin.

—I stand halfway between tears
and stony dry eyes.

You, my brother— and I are
empty handed— soft fear swirls
between us— the companionship
of childhood made solitary on
this day.

I wonder— what next? —and
shift my shoulders over my feet.

You, my brother— turn your
head— our aunt's hand nudges a
whisper.

I step forward— as if in a
dream— to the other side of the
grave where so many bouquets
and wreaths lie.

No one passes me flowers—

I move slowly to where the
flowers are strewn and look and
look— for the right flower.

In my mind then comes a phrase
I'd written once in a story— *In*
China white is the colour of death.

I stand over a bouquet of white
chrysanthemums— remembering
learning to spell and say the
word with as many letters as
petals—

the chrysanthemum— is also a
flower of death— and so I bend
and twist a stem which breaks
unwillingly—

—and place it beside the roses on
the coffin.

ambitions

Woollomooloo, the harbour,
a hotel with green tiles
half way up the wall
and a long bar inside
ringed by ten a.m. drinkers.

The sun in winter is warm
in Sydney and I see you
walking through the Domain
beside me. You are sixteen,
your friend, Val, is fourteen.

You are training to be
commercial artists at East
Sydney Tech. You've told
me the story many times,
but this time I feel your

young presence beside me.
You sit at a long wooden
bench, lettering in your
fine copperplate hand. You
and Val share a joke

or some kind of mischief.
You are the hit of parties
and any chance to dress up,
play dramatics, finds you there
in the midst of it.

But then the war came.
You had no time to be the
artist you wanted to be.
You join the army,
move to South Australia

and ride a horse all day.
You told us that we could not
claim to be horse-women
until we'd fallen two hundred
and sixty-nine times.

In the army, you also learn
to type, to be an efficient
secretary. But the years
muddle for me, and the next
thread I can find takes you

back to Melbourne. You told
me you were offered the
position as Secretary for the
Department of Agriculture
with its total of three staff.

I wonder at the life you'd
have lived in another time.
Artist, economist, politician.
Instead you fell for the farmer
in his shining Tiger Moth.

ii

Tumbarumba, mountains,
an annual rodeo each
New Year and an annual
Bachelors and Spinsters Ball.
This was where you met.

He flew in, tall, dark-
moustached and handsome.
The Tiger Moth circled
once over the town and
landed in the paddock

just beyond its borders.
Curious, you asked who
he was. I imagine you
danced that night at the
Bachelors and Spinsters.

He taught me to Charleston,
and no doubt you were
impressed. Here was a man
who would have been an
engineer, who was an

aviator (he flew the VIPs
around in the war), and
who ran a farm. A self-
sufficient man. You
imagined a life together.

You told me later that you
spent your first years
together in the air. Attended
every air show, every
gathering you could.

There is a photograph of
you both. You are the only
woman in the group. The
wind blows your hair and
the Tiger Moth hunches

in the background. In the
next photograph I can date
you are pregnant. You're
wearing jodhpurs, a riding hat,
and your coat's buttons are

ready to burst. Your final act
before motherhood claimed the
rest of your life was to chase a fire
engine through the streets of
Temora. It's too late to ask you why.

fragments

A week after your death
a small yellow rose—
life on my balcony.

As the cold wraps itself around me
I wonder when I will believe in your death.
It is like believing that winter
will last forever.

The sea whispers secrets in my ears.
Loss, it says. And gain.

The bird stabs the crab with its long beak.
Loss. And gain, says the sea.

Memory is trampled by daily life
        in Melbourne, but

        in Sydney I sit
next to your spirit

        and together
we ride the underground.

sacrifice

In ancient Mexico they stood on
the windy heights of stone grey pyramids,
making offerings to the
god of death—

they tore open the chest
and cut out the heart.

Today, in Melbourne,
I stood on the corner of a windy grey street,
making an offering to the
goddess of love—

I tore open the chest
and cut out my heart.

the dead

i

The dead press their faces up against mine.
They speak to me endlessly of the past.

Souls clamour as I near the
caterwauling realm of the dead.

I seek my mother, but cannot
find her in this murky-aired vault.

They speak to me. They tell me stories
of their lives. But all I want is to speak with her.

They say, *First you must listen to us, you*
must hear our grief. Then you are free

to speak with her. The bench is hard. I will
not eat of the food of the dead. This much I

have already learned. The table is filled
with fruit: apples, pomegranate, plums,

grapes, wild roses. Red onions, carrots,
plaited bread and a glass of red wine

are left to tempt me. The storytellers take
their places around the table and begin.

ii

My name is Charlotte. She brushes back her
corn blond hair. *My mother, her sister,*

my great-grandmother, my great-great uncle,
my great uncle and much later my mother's mother,

my grandmother all perished by their own hand.
Despair was inherited with the blood of my family.

I was the last. They came and took me away,
took me to the camps, where their final kindness

was to end the family curse. There they gassed me,
along with thousands of others. But they could not kill

my spirit, my life which lives on in the thousands
of paintings I made. The theatre of my life.

iii
My name is Anonymous. I speak for all the other
women whose names are unknown, but whose

stories reverberate around these rooms like
thunderous storms. I am not long dead,

my memories still torment me. I stand in a crowd
of tearful women, waiting and wailing. Willing

that the lives of our fathers, brothers, husbands
be spared, or if they are dead, that they did not die

cruelly. The veil of a woman screams with her expired
breath, seeing the names of those she loves on the list.

Those of us who wait, who return to wait again and again
shiver, wanting and not wanting to know.

I return to my daughters in the camp and resolve to flee
into the Afghani mountains when the list bearing

my beloved's name is nailed to the gate. My daughters
and I will run between the flying bullets.

iv
I found freedom in the underworld, where circus
jesters, acrobats and long-limbed stilt walkers play

Russian roulette with their souls. I hardly recognise her.
Is that you? Is that really you? I ask, repeating the question.

Fire breathing women walk by, each question punctuated
by a flaring of the mouth. Her soul retreats again

and I reach out to grab her hand. Death is wheeled by
on a cart such as Athena once invented. The underworld

is not technologically literate, but a primitive world
full of primitive passions. Death casts her eye over me

and passes on. Not yet. Not for me, at least. There she
is again. *Mum,* I call. She turns, her eyes owl-grey,

where once they shone blue. A beach ball flies
between us, light as a ghost. I hold her hand, cold,

and press it to my hairline. Her gaze passes over
my left shoulder and I wonder who she sees. I want

to talk, but no speech can creep between my lips.
When her mouth opens, I see neon words fly like birds

but no sound … I strain to hear but there are only the
faint strains of an accordion, like a circus passing by

on a distant road. She makes the leap as Death cruises
past again and takes her place on the horse-drawn

cart. No backward glance, no regret, simply passing on.
As I turn to leave the world of the dead, my eyes catch

another face I know. No warning and the dead throttle
past me in their rush for eternity.

v

And another and another. Is there no end to the greed
of Death? Crossing the road in her prime, Death

steers straight for her. Didn't she notice? Did neither
notice? Death did. Death stood by the bed for days.

Pushed and pulled by life's will. But Death is a bad loser,
knowing that her endurance outlasts all.

I spin the wheel waiting for the next game.
A pomegranate rudely torn open tempts me, a glass

of red wine is proffered. Souls bristle into the seats nearby,
the storytellers take their place around the table and begin …

May 1994–October 1996

india sutra

india sutra[1]

For Hugh David Hawthorne
31 Jan 1913 to 28 Jan 2004
and for travelling companions,
Lariane and Renate

Prologue
They say that in ancient times
women didn't travel,

but I, Avis, say they did.
Women travelled in pairs

across the Australian desert,
Isis sailed the Nile,

the seven girls became birds,
took flight heading skywards, Amazons

rode horses, protecting their lands,
Medea, Helen, Sita and others

not yet known to us travelled for love.
So why not ancient lesbians?

In this time lesbians travel
for love. Our relationships

span continents, cross oceans
and gather frequent flyer points,

1 *Sutra*. Literally, a string or thread. Also a literary form.

modern day swan-maidens.
Here are three voices:

Sakhi from India, displaced
at fourteen to a land where

the secular rites of cricket
and football take the place

of gods, mandalas
and yonis carved in stone.

Sakhi is on a quest for
an identity both elusive

and forbidden. She is searching
for a lost recipe and hoping

to catch it in a photograph.
Leda is of European descent.

One day I called her Scintl
and it stuck. She says,

I am no Leda, I refuse to represent
dead Europa. She longs for India

as for something lost, some
quality of life, some release.

Will this trip ring out the end?

Will her knees hold up?

Her wings rustle with uncertainty,
but Scintl's humour keeps her walking.

Then there is Avis who longs
only to fly, who in attending

one meeting in India, is missing
another in Melbourne where

she is the black sheep, the crow
who cannot cease speaking

the awful truth. Avis is a poet born
in the town named for its crows.

For each, a longing,
for each, a release.

The plans are made, the tickets
booked. Three women

caught in a mix of cultures
rehearsing imagined futures.

28 Dec 2003, Bingil Bay
Avis: I dream of mortality.
My father not yet dead,

the coffin missing
but still they try to bury him.

Seven ages of men buried beneath the flag,
he's not ready yet,

not dead yet,
and the coffin is not built.

Bingil Bay
Scintl: A troubling dream,
an operating theatre filled

with masked women and men.
They open my knee

only to find the plastic
and steel has dissolved.

I wake to a ragdoll knee
unable to walk.

Geelong
Sakhi: I dream of Chowpatty Beach,
the recipe for bhel puri has been stolen.

I go in search of it all over India.
I interview thousands and no one

can remember it. In the end
they tell me it has never existed.

first sutra

16 Jan 2004, Mumbai
India raises its nuclear hand
and so does Pakistan

but on this stage in Mumbai
a single stage

the band Jinoon blasts out peace
Pakistani rock rocks Mumbai.

o

From the parade ground
a lakh of souls watch and listen

Debating imperialism is like debating
the pros and cons of rape, says Arundhati

Roy. Her absolution, she says,
is to be allowed into Frying Pan Park[2]

2 In her opening speech at the World Social Forum, Mumbai on 16 January 2004 Arundhati Roy spoke of the annual Thanksgiving Day pardon of a single turkey by the US President. One turkey is pardoned but fifty million turkeys are slaughtered. "That's how New Racism in the corporate era works. A few carefully bred turkeys – the local elites of various countries, a community of wealthy immigrants, investments bankers, the occasional Colin Powell, or Condoleeza Rice, some singers, some writers (like myself) – are given absolution, and a pass to Frying Pan Park."

unlike the others, she talks turkey
with the condemned turkeys.

o

Manjula, thirteen years old,
and Vice-President of Bhima Sangha,

laughs with her eight- and ten-year-old
friends, ragpickers all of them,

she smiles into the camera.
Small fry, condemned to be

a turkey, forever scratching
through the rags of others.

17 Jan
We— Sakhi, Scintl and I,
(Avis of the crows)

begin the day with masala
dosa, crunching it into being.

o

We're at the gates of another world,
Cerberus is here, so too

the old guard and the avant garde
The grounds are abuzz with banners, leaflets,

drummers beat out a rhythm for the
protestors, some sing, some dance

GLOBALISE HUMAN RIGHTS.
MUSLIM WOMEN & SEXUALITY.

ORISSA ADIVASI ADHIKA
NO COMPANIES, NO CORPORATES

ONLY COMMUNITIES CONTROL
OVER LAND FORESTS AND OCEANS.

GLOBALISATION IS A QUESTION,
DALITS ARE THE QUESTION MARK.

WOMEN IN BLACK AGAINST WAR.
NATIONAL DISABILITY NETWORK.

IF ANOTHER WORLD IS POSSIBLE
MAKE TIBET A ZONE OF PEACE.

WHO WOULDN'T DIE TO WEAR A SHAHTOOSH
SAY NO TO SHAHTOOSH.

Each brings to the event her own hopes,
her stories of hardship and action.

For me, it's a dream turned reality.
My theories tested in the dry dust

of Mumbai. Here, if anywhere,
perhaps another world is possible.

o

A buzz of black and yellow
padmini cabs swarm toward me

in the late afternoon sun
dancing into the lucrative hive

so many customers
from so many places

the negotiations spiral
toward the vein of honey.

A thousand rupees …
Four hundred rupees …

Eight hundred …
Four hundred and fifty …

Six hundred rupees …
Five hundred.

And the queen makes the deal.

o

The flute-seller carries
his wooden pipes

an echidna's spines
humped on his back

his tune calling
each passer-by

each child dancing behind
the pied piper.

My lens is fractured,
what I see, like the colonisers before me,

comes through the eyes of a different
geography a world of other fauna.

But India and Australia share a substratum,
Gondwanaland.

18 Jan
We ride in the ladies-only carriage
to Goregaon. Crushed body to body.

Above the fans whirr hot air, below
our feet the rails zing with electricity.

Women board selling from trays
earings, hair clasps, ribbons.

Disgorged at the other end,
Scintl, friend of Cerberus,

stops to photograph dogs
lazing on railway roofs.

Mementos for Sindhu, she says,
since she can't be with us.

We need a world that's
friendly for dogs too.

o

A sarong covers my head
I throw up behind its wrap.

A group of men in white
jalabas look at me,

I care nothing for their stares.
My head pounds, like the pounding

of old Sisyphus tumbling
headlong down the rocky slope.

My body removes itself
from the pain, taking flight,

I stand, wobble into the crowd
of Dalits proclaiming on the backs

of their jackets that it is they, Dalits,
who will make another world possible.

Right now, all I want is a world
in which migraines are impossible.

19 Jan
I walk to the workshop
B42, says the program.

It's at the edge of the grounds
a marginal place to talk about

a marginal group, lesbians
beaten, killed, jailed, ostracised

tortured because of love
I find B45, B44, B43 … B41?

Where is B42? Is this a metaphor
for our invisibility?

o

We begin to talk. The students
of psychology speak about delinquent girls

whom they hope to rehabilitate
so they might marry, be normal girls.

When I speak, what do they hear?
Am I the Dalit? Am I untouchable

in another way?
I say, *What of the trauma?*

What of the suicides? The silences?
They hear my words

but not the silence between us.
In spite of this, we build small trust

through conversation. We speak of
the insults and assaults

encountered in the countries
represented by these twenty women.

It's a women-only session, I say
to the man at the door.

It's Ganesh in drag,
neither here nor there.

I repeat my sentence, and as I do
some women inside the door

rise to leave. Small trust is shattered,
openness ruptured into fragility.

We begin again,
shuffling into speech.

They burned the house of
a couple in Kerala, says one.

They flog the women in my country,
says another from Iran.

In Cuba, I cannot speak, there I cannot exist,
says the Canadian activist.

Each knows the precarious
existence of the world

she inhabits, of the world
which claims another world is possible.

But even in this tent at the margins
of possibility, that possible world remains elusive.

o

A rainbow of protestors gather
each pinned with a multicoloured badge.

HIJRAS[3] ARE WOMEN, says the banner.
But, I ask, *Are lesbians people?*

No hijras attend the session on
Muslim Women & Sexuality.

Is that because
hijras are also men?

o

The tongue is silent, still we
cannot speak, cannot name ourselves.

3 Hijras have played a social role in Indian society for many years. Traditionally hijras are eunuch men. These days the definition of hijra is broader and includes men who are gay, transsexual or cross-dressers.

Is this what freedom amounts to?

O

Later, at the hotel,
I mull over my invisibility,

my untouchability.
The migraine recedes,

into its shadowlife.
Temporary relief.

I am back in my body again.
What a surprising experience!

20 Jan
Who is at the door?
Is it Ganesh, doorkeeper

to the women's quarters,
the world of women

who from their own fluids
give birth to the elephant-headed one

neither male nor female.
Perhaps it was Ganesh who wrote the

T-shirt slogan,
Heterosexuality isn't normal – just common.

o

Scintl is in the midst of debates on IVF,
infanticide of girls, stem-cell selection

and cloning, I can almost hear
her feathers ruffling the canvas-walled room.

Between words she passes the old
fruit bar from the airline,

suddenly hunger takes me.
I chew through the remainder

until with a nudge of wings
she insists I share.

o

The women's toilet has a queue
outside the door, where a sign reads,

Hurry up!
2.4 million people want to use the toilet.

o

Here we sit, activists from
four continents, five corners

one chair empty, a reminder of
our visa-less friend. *Allowed out,*

they say, *but not back*. The risk
is that she'll speak out of line

in this global line dance.
I talk through the jarring

jackhammer; through the migraine
still hammering my skull.

21 Jan
Chowpatty Beach is home
to Sakhi's childhood memories

We've been filling up on bhel puri daily,
tasting the past on your tongue.

In the night's warm air we watch as chefs
in high hats and red gingham aprons

cook up scents of coriander,
mint and lemon mixed with ginger,

tamarind, onion and chilli.

o

Scintl dreams of returning
to this world as a cockatoo,

she dreams of a life without pain,
without papers and files,

knees that can take sudden landings.
Is any other world possible?

o

Why would a knife sharpener
ply his trade at two a.m.

unless his tools were made in hell
and he knew that with each screech

of metal on metal
the migraine would burn itself

deeper into your brain?

22 Jan, Pune
We're on the road,
heading south.

Observe lane discipline,
says the road sign.

Yoga for the road.

o

In the Tribal Museum
Scintl and I are welcomed by

a lollypink mask,
warli paintings bloom

white on ochre
a drummer and dancing figures

a snake encircling a tree trunk.
Paradise? An Indian

Garden of Eden?
Scenes of harmony

a chowk, a goddess
at the centre.

Some other time
another world was possible.

Was it in the days when
Urvashi and Puruvas

were as elusive as the wind?[4]
When Sappho was not only

the tenth muse, but also
a black swan, a white cow

before all the swans were white
and Europa was raped?

o

The sweet shop sells cakes
depicting scenes of cricket

4 For more on these mythic figures, see Giti Thadani. 1996. *Sakhiyani: Lesbian Desire in Ancient and Modern India*, pp. 38-45.

green icing, an orange crease.
Small men in white stand

poised to bat in front of
pink-topped wickets.

We wander into an arcade
to explore the worlds of women,

to touch the fabrics, to wonder at
the vibrant colours of two silken saris.

But a crowd blocks our path.
It's India versus Australia.

Twenty minutes of play until tea.

o

23 Jan
Pune, the place of hard beds
my hips eroded by sleep

I wake with muscles aching,
they have contracted in fear overnight.

Has my body absconded again?
Unlike me, Scintl rises without

shattering pain in her knees.
For now her knees are taking the pace.

o

The woman holds out her hands,
blunted by leprosy.

Her eyes shine.
She takes the coin in her scarf.

Would I, could I …?

o

Sunnydale and Sakhi. More memories.
your mother's, your aunt's

your grandparents' too.
It's where your father

wooed your mother
over years. Such patience.

But the world has changed and
no one believes in the future any more.

We three walk the Pune streets,
past the school yard, past the sweet shop,

and your memories are tumbling out
in pictures and stories as we walk.

The living-room at Aunty Esme's
Sunnydale is filled with mementos.

A flying duck takes off on the wall
above Aunty Esme's head,

the floral décor lights up next to
a lute-playing angel, and Christ's

head, though crowned with thorns,
is surrounded by a string of silver stars.

On the wall, a doily, family photographs,
a pink cardboard model house

perched above a tea-towel
printed with Christmas motifs.

The tiles at my feet create
3D optical illusions.

A decorated fish graces the table,
food preparation a ritual for guests

fish-scales made of Spanish onion.
After dinner there are games

to make the family and visitors laugh.
In my family, in Scintli's family,

we both would not play. The distance
here is far enough removed

to let it be. But I see the familiar
rebellions on Sakhi's face.

o

This headache is like a string,
beading the days together,

creating patterns of pain,
my head a temple to pain.

o

It was Lakshmi who wished
Vishnu's head to fall from his neck

in a fit of fury. Born of ocean
with a lotus crowning her head

her body is a petalled rose
hidden in the darkest cave.

Our rebellions too, lie hidden,
as we each negotiate our place

in the father worlds, the brother worlds,
the husband worlds. I hear Sakhi

fumbling answers to the questions.
And you have a son?

But no husband?

24 Jan
The colour of poverty
is charcoal brown,

streaked with aquamarine,
magenta and yellow.

o

Yervada, a palace built
by the Agha Khan,

the walls like sugar candy,
tangerine and white,

now a shrine of devotion
to Mahatma Gandhi

also his wife, far less known
Kasturba Gandhi.

We visit with you, Sakhi, the
granddaughter of Gandhi's jailer.

Your camera is creating memories
but the jailers now want to arrest you

for pointing your eyes, your camera
in the wrong direction.

25 Jan
We talk of place, of migration,
of belonging and of the ways

identity shapes us. You now find
your parental culture far less strange.

Transplanted, the social context
ripped away, Catholic devotions

made no sense in secular Australia.
Here in India, it is just one of many paths

to heaven. *Second-generation longing,*
that's what it is, I say. In India,

I discover the source of my mother's
nostalgia for the west coast of Scotland.

o

We travel overnight to
Aunty Thecla's, your

mother's best friend.
We're on the Goa King,

the royalty of sleeper buses.
Seats flattened to beds,

like the ads for
British Airways Business.

The fantasy of comfort
confronts reality when

my hip crunches against the metal bar
there to keep me from bouncing to the floor.

Passengers have been known to bounce
right out of bed onto the road.

26 Jan, Goa
Aunty Thecla, headmistress of the Catholic school
has a routine that includes daily mass,

overseeing the school and maintaining
social connections. These rituals of piety

spell out schoolgirl discomfort, forced attendance,
a history in which church and education

are too close. As in Pune, Aunty Thecla's
whole existence is so embedded that

my habitual discomforts dissolve—
and then I discover her subversive wit.

And I tell you who is thriving.
The coffin maker.

He has three trucks now.
So says Aunty Thecla

o

Happiness is a dry fart,
says the Lonely Planet guide to India,

And I say,
It's not natural to walk with a tightened sphincter.

27 Jan
Old Goa, a slice of inquisitorial
Portugal-invaded India.

St Francis Xavier, minus his
big toe, lies here. Every ten years

the crowds come to gawk
at this European relic.

Gold and gilt surround
his images at the Se Cathedral.

o

I purchase a plastic
gold-trimmed replica

for my friend, a collector
of tourist altar pieces.

A prayer for the sinful,
quips Scintl.

o

Is that Satan staring down from
the yellow-horned blue mask?

At the spice plantation
they ply us with food,

crab curry, kokum, rafi,
kadhi patha. An old man

rolls bidis for the tourists
to smoke. A young man

demonstrates coconut palm
climbing, limbs leaping.

Soon I'm swinging from a vine
like an orang utan.

o

Did you know
10,000 lesbians

are descending on Goa
for a convention?

And at the invitation
of the Indian government!

What is the world coming to?
My eyes light up, Sakhi sinks

into the couch. It's Scintl
who asks simply, *When?*

Aunty Thecla changes the subject.

o

In *Sakhiyani*, Giti Thadani
writes of Sarasvati, goddess

of knowledge, reclaiming
the Vedas, reinstating

a chain of feminine genealogies.
She invokes the two bright cows,

wandering women who graze
and suckle, lick and caress,

their bodies newly woven
with oceanic light.[5]

o

The river sings, bubbling
words into speech

from speech comes lyric poetry
sung by young women

5 Giti Thadani. 1996. *Sakhiyani*, pp. 16-32.

in the service of Sappho
sister to Saraswati

who wrote her world
into existence, memory

inscribed on stone, on palm leaf
and she carried fire

underwater, underground
where she flows invisibly

more sacred than the things
that can be seen

lapis -> halapis -> salapis -> sarapis ->
sarapphis -> sarappha -> sappha -> psappha

sarappha -> sarapfa -> sarapva -> sarapwa ->
sarahapwa -> saraswa -> saraswati -> savoir

28 Jan
In India the animals have road sense.
The buffalo cross the street in double file.

The dogs look both ways before they cross.
Even the goats keep in formation.

And in the paddy fields
herons practise geometry.

The buffalo is in camouflage, wearing
green vegetation across its back.

o

The waiter brings food piled high,
pomfret in Goan spices,

blue and yellow lobster, cream-filled,
and a delicacy of prawns.

Over food we talk of home,
of friendships under duress.

Let's gather all our troubles and
drown them in a gunny sack.

o

Gunny sack, says Sakhi
and I think of my father's

khaki war paraphernalia.
The Tiger Moth

with its spare engine,
the silk maps of the

New Guinea Highlands,
the arsenic pill, just in case,

eight hundred pairs of army issue
cotton khaki undershorts.

And then there are the endless
collections of tools,

the river pump (and no river)
three compressors,

five jacks. A header
agisted down the road

for twenty years. He is
a hoarder of hardware.

For my mother it was
books and letters,

birds and paintings.
But she is gone.

And he? He remembers the war years,
the best years of his life.

Three years ago I cleared out the
old house, learned about my forebears

through photographs, found another
path to myself. Much of it

excess baggage. Metal
recycled for a new life.

o

In Goa, tourists tear along on
motorcycles, ignoring the tacit

road rules. At Anjuna market,
everyone has something to sell,

spices, dolls, embroidered fabrics. From the
Rajasthani woman I buy a cylindrical

woven hat, zig-zagged with colour
that perches atop my head.

o

Aunty Thecla and I share
a discerning palate.

She, more catholic than the pope,
me, more pagan than Sappho.

Like me, she peels the pith
from the segments of orange,

she spits out the pips of grapes,
and her favourite food is pasta.

During the telling of stories,
I realise that the headache

has finally lifted, post-migraine
élan drives through me,

I say, *It's done, it's gone,*
I'll be okay now.

o

I go to bed, check my mobile.
There's a message. My sister.

My father.
My father has died.

Three days short of his
ninety-first birthday.

One month after my dream and
a day filled with memories of him.

29 Jan
The day is swinging out of view
I'm caught in limbo

I can't reach my sister.
It's four a.m. in Australia.

At eight a.m. her phone is engaged.
Perhaps a message to western China

to my niece. Or to my brother.
I begin to write an sms,

just then, I receive one from him.
I'm in America. WRU?

Five of us are out of the country.
I ring my aunt. I ring my sister.

Still engaged. I ring her work.
She's not there.

I fall into a dishevelled sleep.
Later, we talk. My sister and I.

o

She was with him on the weekend.
His last weekend.

He celebrated with beer and angels tears
for lunch two days in a row.

There are some calories in it,
muses my sister.

The sun sets over the river's mouth
at Panjim. Scintl and I walk to

The Quarterdeck, order
bottle of Kingfisher beer

and drink to my father's spirit.

30 Jan
In Ponda they prepare for
a February festival. The ten-metre

high oil lamp is polished,
the cobra-headed palanquins

are painted, the women sell
necklaces of marigold woven

with bougainvillea. The dogs
sleep in plastic chairs, sniffing incense.

o

There's a temple on the border
between Goa and Karnataka

the Mahadevi Temple,
built in honour of a queen.

Fashioned of black basalt
from the far side of the Ghats.

Built in the Kadamba period,
it was a time of peace.

Not just a decade or two,
but three hundred years.

The clues are engraved into the temple.
It is ringed with vulvic symbols,

entwined double snakes,
spirals, petalled stone.

o

That's it, says Sakhi.
I'm over that identity stuff.

I want to interview lesbians.
I want to find the recipe

for bhel puri.

o

31 Jan, Kerala
Known for sailing to India,
Vasco da Gama

died here in Fort Kochin.
On this westering point he has

the best view of the setting sun
of anyone, anywhere.

Cantilevered Chinese fishing nets
from the time of Kublai Khan

stretch like giant praying mantises
toward the sinking golden bauble.

o

Today could have been
his ninety-first birthday.

A seventeenth-century
Scottish forebear called

Solomon is the earliest trace
of my father's ancestry.

Two thousand years ago
Jews travelled to Kochin.

A Hebrew sign fronts an ancient
cemetery, the Paradesi Synagogue

is still in use, but most have migrated
back to Israel, leaving only

windows framed with the Star of David,
and fourteen Jews in Jew Town.

1 Feb
In *The Hindu* I read my stars.
Here the archer is called Dhanus.

Does Dhanus fling arrows
into the sky? Or are the

eighteen stars of the moon's
mansions— Moola,

Poorvashada and Uttarshada—
fireworks enough?

O

We climb the mountain
behind lumbering trucks,

dodge the hurtling buses
on the downhill.

How the sharp-ridged
copper snake survives

its road crossings,
we'll never know.

We stop to look at
manicured tea plantations

where women pluck each leaf.
In Munnar metal kitchen-wares

are strung like jewels,
mannequins are hung with garments,

the market-place pulses with
fresh vegetables and fruits.

A blue-shirted boy poses
in his carefully stocked stall.

2 Feb
The Catholic church has
perfected the art of façades.

At the roadside an elephant
dresses for temple.

Three religions battle for supremacy
in the hill station of Munnar.

The Catholic church graces
the highest point.

The Hindu temple and Islamic mosque
straddle the slopes below.

On the main street a store sign reads,
Dealers in Agricultural Inputs.

The religion of markets now
has a foothold in India.

o

We head west toward the backwaters.
Water pervades the language,

Malayalam, Kerala, Malabar,
filled with liquids.

Kettavaalum ply
the liminal edges of memory.

Mourning my father,
the stillness is made solid by

the white heron standing amidst
the purple water hyacinth.

Low slung bungalows,
covered by tropical foliage,

hide behind walls painted
with the hammer and sickle.

3 Feb, Mammalapuram
Chennai Airport has
a Ladies Refusal Room.

Who is refusing whom?

o

On the beach at Mammalapuram,
boats are strewn at the water's edge.

Men are fixing nets.
Women selling sarongs.

Puppies playing in the sand.
Who said anything about innocence?

o

Playing ocean and boat.

I am a floating boat
I am a drunken boat

I am a drowned boat
I am a sunken boat

Playing ocean and boat.

o

Home of the *Mahabharata*
10,000 verses devoted to battle

memorialised in the five rathas
the first dedicated to Kali

whose people speak
the language of birds.

They dance and sing their life away,
some even to the gallows.

We each carry our demons:
for Scintl it is the demon work

the betrayals of the thugs
of respectability and liberalism

who strangle silently from behind;
for Sakhi they are demons of culture

of battles between the freedoms
of the West and the riches

of India, again these demons
are quiet stranglers with silken cloths;

even circus can become a demon
and Avis has had her wings clipped

she cannot fly, she cannot write,
she knows the meetings held

in her absence will crucify her
one more time, will endorse

invisibility and create
false histories.

o

Kali's press is bad.
A tangle of red flowers

fall about the shoulders
of the demons who chew

on children. Like most mothers
Kali tries to save her children

from demons reproducing like rabbits.
A bloodbath ensues.

In defence she invents
the stealthy ambush of the thugs,

men who strangle demons
silently, bloodlessly.[6]

O

At the Cave Temple
rocks imitate elephants

rocks take on the female form,
vulval and clitoral.

Enigmatic tracks are carved
across the rock face

leading us back to the cave
where Lakshmi swings her hips

and settles her feathers as
lotus petal and swan morph.

Dali might have been here
with his liquid eye, a place

where swan, elephant and dragon
merge in giant sculptural forms.

6 Kevin Rushby. 2003. *Children of Kali*.

4 Feb
In this one speeding car, we feel unsafe.
Perhaps the driver has a contract

with Kali whose flower,
the red hibiscus, adorns the dashboard

of the Ambassador taxi. Around
the country are bleeding places.

Places sacred to Kali.
At Vrindyachul Kali's

breast fell to the ground.
In Assam at Kamkhya,

where her vagina landed,
the earth menstruates every July.

5 Feb
I dream I'm going up
inside a mountain.

Carcasses of dead sheep are
strewn along the spiral way.

I wake thinking of him again.
The sheep's carcass hanging

from the branch of the old eucalypt.
The blood draining. His method kosher.

And he is flying through the mountains
of New Guinea, the first to land on

airstrips in the highlands. *Like*
landing on a field of pumpkins,

he said. Or riding out a blown tyre
on the coral airstrip of Horn Island.

The epitaph is ready, written for both.
My mother, the whistler who

dreamed of flight, who collected birds.
My father, the pilot. The one she met

at the Bachelors and Spinsters Ball.
He circled the paddock at Tumbarrumba

three times. This landing a cinch.
His Tiger Moth would become

well known on the western slopes
of New South Wales.

May their spirits soar.

o

In Mammalapuram I purchase a Ladakhi
thanka from a young Kashmiri man.

We drink mint tea, and Sakhi is
haggling the price. In business

I can haggle too, but not here.
It's the distance again,

this time stopping me, creating
that tourist discomfort.

o

In Ladakh they paint *thankas*
a universe filled with spirit

a body rich with chakras
in a land dry as the Sahara.

We all stand on the floating lotus
fish-footed, our calves as tough

as tortoises, our thighs as strong
as mares. The kundalini snake is

coiled to rise, fast as an otter
at the sun centre. An

enlightened soul sits astride
a cow in the centre of

the Star of David. Or is it
a Tibetan mandala?

A hare crouches at the throat,
her petalled brain is horn-headed

and golden dragons circle
Chomo-Lung Ma, mother

of the universe, the highest
sky you'll ever reach.

6 Feb

In all of India, the place
most sacred is the confluence of

three rivers, goddess rivers.
The two above flow east,

the third, Saraswati, underground
and invisible, flows west.

Saraswati invented flowing
words, the speech of rivers,

syllables etched on hennaed hands.
Here bodies are burned and float

down river in their catafalques.
People dream of dying here,

of floating into the realm
that follows life.

No such journey will await
my father. The Murrumbidgee's

broad swathe is no highway
for funerary rites.

o

The full moon is rising in the east,
rising above the wavy horizon.

The sea laps our feet. In the
morning the boats will push off

their nets thrown, fish caught
and the cycle begins again.

The moon engraves our three faces
looking eastward on this final night.

One moon in the cycle of the year,
one of twelve moons – or is it thirteen?

13 Feb, Wagga Wagga
The three of us— Sakhi, Scintl and I—
have driven up for my father's funeral.

Will my relatives be as hospitable?
We sit in the second pew,

a row of women, I turn my head and count,
in this row most of us are lesbians.

My sister, my brother, husbands and wives
are in the front row. Is this an accident?

Or some truism of social invisibility
that binds the world? The one that is possible.

o

In Wagga Wagga, the place
of many crows, the place

of my birth, the place of
my father's death,

we gather to celebrate your life.
As if still alive, you sweat

in the forty-degree heat.
But what is that against flying

in New Guinea where
the clouds have rocks in them?

What is that when
you could put on a falsetto

under your black-waxed moustache
the day they picked you to play

the Fair Maiden?
What is that when

you could pull apart
a combine harvester,

spread it out in the paddock
and put it back together again?

What is that against
thirteen hours perched

in a tree above raging floodwaters,
sleeping intermittently,

strapped on only
by your trouser belt?

What is that for the man
who could romance

from a Tiger Moth?
They lay poppies for you,

and the last post
sounds for the last time.

o

Avis: *Another world? No, this one.*
In Melbourne they formalised

my end and imagined a future
so weird I could only laugh.

My father's end was peaceful,
what more can one hope for?

Scintl: *The ragdoll knees are gone,*
the pain remains but my knees

can walk on, just as I walked India.
Today I cancelled the operation.

Sakhi: *I've found those who remember*
the recipe, they know it exists.

second sutra

26 May 2004, Delhi
Scintl, for all her dreams of future
bird flight, hates the turbulence of

human flight. *Where is your cockatoo*
self tonight Scintli? I ask. *Maybe*

in your next life the air will be smooth.
Lightning forks outside the plane,

as we come in to land at Delhi airport.
If there is one, says Scintl.

How will it be this time,
without the eyes, the stories of Sakhi?

o

During the drive to the hotel I am hit by
a wave of familiarity. The tuk-tuks,

the Tata-owned trucks, the government-
of-India blue signs, the atmosphere.

It is like coming home. Australia and India,
colonial outposts of the British,

have much in common. But I am
no local, nor a tourist guide.

This time I'm here as companion
to hard-working Scintl.

o

27 May
The tangle of nature and culture,
animal and human are

two intersecting triangles.
Indian love-birds,

triangulating, beak to beak
on the mural that fronts

the hospital for birds
at the centre of Old Delhi.

The sounds of vendors
breaking into this oasis.

Even the boys with slingshots
have their place amid the electrical

towers, the buses and the bird
doctors in their white coats.

o

This city pulsates. It's blood
through a catheter. The natural

half contained. Pot plants flower
from the back of a bicycle, a silver-

dressed mannequin glitters on a raised
catwalk, supported by cold metal and

coiled wires. The sun shadows through
the cracks revealing a man in high shoes,

folds of coloured fabrics, a pyramid of
dried beans, rolls of sisal rope.

o

The women are far less visible.
I follow donkeys down even

narrower lanes, behind the main
thoroughfare where daily lives

are lived. Here is the pulsing heart,
uncontained. Broccoli, capsicum,

carrot and chilli. Here is the woman
in her store selling every knick-knack

you ever imagined. Here are the cows
paused in their midday meditations.

Here is sixty-year-old Chandra Kala
smoking her hookah seated on a string bed.

And here am I, Avis, with free days
while Scintli sits in meetings,

drawing up schedules, listing names
for the next big conference.

o

Delhi, like Kampala, like Rome,
is built on sevens. Seven cities,

and maybe more, they say of Delhi.
On a blue door in the old city

a string of lemons and chillies hang.
A charm to repel evil.

o

28 May
At Jagori I am watching a TV screen.
For two months I was catatonic,

I didn't have the voice you hear today …
Women writers gave me voice.

It's Andrea Dworkin in a time warp
from the 1970s speaking in black and white

to this young Indian researcher, spending
her holidays cataloguing the collection.

o

The women of Jagori share lunch
in a circle, seated on the floor.

Come, eat with us, Avis, says Meena.
They run courses for women,

counsel the desperate, keep the
finances in balance, write poetry in Urdu

and computer programs in C+.
They research and speak, digitise

and collect history for the future.
Fourteen years ago I came here.

This woman's face filled with liveliness,
Kadru says, *I could not read or write.*

Now the women come with me
I tell those officers behind the desk

to read the letters themselves.
Why should I read to them?

Kadru's laughter, her sheer vitality
make me want to learn Hindi

on the spot. We may not share a
language, but we could share lunch.

o

There's a note in a file about the
destruction of sacred lesbian sites.

It records the cutting off of breasts,
symbolising what they would do

to living lesbians, if they
could get away with it.

I make a copy for Sakhi.
And I think, has anything changed?

Cultural denial is alive and well.
The natives have no culture,

say the perpetrators of crucifixions.
Lesbians have no culture,

say the apoliticals, pleading
mainstream recognition,

but assimilation results only
in radishes, coconuts, transsexualism,

avoidance behaviour and denial.

o

29 May
We attend a reading in Arabic
and Hindi. I watch the facial

muscles of the two women
as they read, listen to the

rhythms of their voices. It's
not only words we read.

o

30 May, Agra
It's 10.30 a.m. and forty degrees.
The most poetic ad for Fosters

greets us at the hotel: *Tastes like*
an angel crying on your tongue.

o

But it's not angels that people
my dreams on that first day.

It's the demons again, ghosts
of Kali, circus freaks and

crucifixion disguised as
mediation. Softly softly

the betrayers are there again
angling for banishment.

They will not say it, but it's there
in every part of their demeanour:

there's hypocrisy and cowardice,
two-faced irresponsibility,

there's drunkenness and righteousness
when the quiet execution is performed.

o

The marble cupola nudges
over the wall, the rickshaw

driver pedalling through
the sweat and heat.

Thousands of people pack the lawns,
the stone-edged pools,

shawled from the sun. These people make
it a more human place, a place

of colour, of wind-blown fabric,
of hijras in the brightest gowns of all.

A little girl in pink skips toward me,
her image caught by the wind.

When the shadows are all in
the right place, the photographers

emerge from behind bushes, their bare feet
slapping against the sun-warmed marble.

O

The Kingfisher beer is cold, the roof
terrace warm at dusk. A surreal place

with fantastic chairs bent from bamboo,
an earthenware pot, cactus and

the Taj Mahal billowing behind the
buildings. The family next door

gathers on a daybed. They wave to
these two unknown tourists.

Monkeys carouse in the trees,
pigeons return to their homes,

and young boys fly kites across the sun
setting globular in the haze.

To our loves and losses,
to exile and betrayal, I say.

To the banishment of pain
and to your father, says Scintl.

And we both see the river at Panjim,
the sun setting as the covered boat sails by.

And one for Sakhi and her research.
We laugh, remembering

ten thousand lesbians descending…

o

The night market is a crush
of people. Loud music beats away all

thought. There are food stalls, stalls filled
with bangles, dolls, pots and pans,

ornaments, drinks and bright powders.
He's eight or nine and fancies himself

as a tourist guide. He's learning his trade
in commercial harassment. *This way,*

he says, tugging at my sleeve. I resist and
pull away. But he does not give up.

He trails me to breaking point,
shadows the wall, smiles with satisfaction

until we climb into another rickshaw
and leave the kite festival streets.

o

31 May
Old Agra is shimmering in the heat.
A dozen or more handmade ladders

lean against the awnings. Horses, cows,
motorbikes, bicycles, trucks are pumped

through these narrow streets. The
heart in a drawn out systole.

Scintl and I pause for chai.
Around us men, they watch us

and we watch them. Boiled water
into tin cups, rinsed and only then

the chai. Wearing other eyes
we are like technicolour movie

cut outs in a medieval marketplace
filmed in black and white.

Ornately carved balconies jut above
a yellow wall proclaiming

BUTTER
utterly butterly delicious. A man,

head covered like a penitent, walks the
street in platform shoes. Bamboo

creates the most original retail scaffold
for bright pink, green and yellow

girls' dresses. In this world of multiple
zones time is never in the same place.

Centuries contained in a single gaze.
Metal-wheeled carts front shops with

internet access; carved stone dogs
guard Coca-Cola; saris and cigarettes

are sold by the same man.
At the station the shoeshiners,

grounded by broken limbs,
delight in false repairs.

But it's the thirsty cows who have
the last say, tethered close

they low and drink
one another's urine

beside the river
refracting oceanic light.

o

In Agra, I hope I have left behind
the shuddering tears of anger.

Knocked sideways by this rush
of women into a vacuum of power.

I confront them with a history
they neither know nor recognise.

Even now they do not wish
to hear me speak.

o

1 June, Delhi
Delhi seems quiet after Agra.
From the house of our friend

Scintl and I catch a tuk-tuk
to the shops in search of some

elusive souvenir not available
in the global market place.

On Connaught Place, we savour
the flavour of real global coffee.

The evening finds us eating
dosa again, down a lane

through a maze of streets
that only a local could unravel.

It's our souls unravelling.
Scintl has become herself again,

energy rising, serpentine Kundalini,
swan wings ready for lift off.

And Avis? She ponders her
vulnerabilities, forgotten

schoolgirl powerlessness,
ostracism and lies.

She vows to get on with it,
to return to Delhi, and to fly.

third sutra

28 Dec 2004, Bingil Bay
It's none of us going to India this time
but India coming to us on screens

as the ocean comes to the people of
Mammalapuram, on the eastern shore.

These poems congeal
and the poets are still not ready.[7]

The shoreline temples, the giant
boulders, the carved elephants

are not enough to hold back
the fury of earth's waters.

Where once was tourism and haggling
is now carnage and despair.

Where is the woman who sold me the sarong?
Where are the men fixing nets?

Where are the children and the puppies?
Where are the shopkeepers,

7 Suniti Namjoshi in her poem "Nov 1970 Cyclone in Pak." asks if the poets could be ready the next time a disaster of this magnitude occurs. And in 1991 she answers her own question saying, that they are not and never can be. Suniti Namjoshi. 1993. *St Suniti and the Dragon*, p. 52.

the young man from Kashmir who sold
the *thanka* that now hangs on my wall?

The shops selling souvenirs
have filled with mud.

The fishing boats and a tangle of nets
are strewn in the streets

and dead fish line the pavements.
Meanwhile, houses and their inhabitants

are drowned at sea.
I can no longer play ocean and boat.

December 2003–March 2005

fragilities

gravity defied

Life's a dance, a dance in
four lines, eight moves
like the tai chi old women practise
on the Bund in Shanghai
or like the twists and
turns of acrobats

In Egypt she spends a whole day
on a camel, riding to Saqqara
the oldest pyramid of all,
she scrambles in the sand just to see the tomb

On a rooftop of a hotel in Jaipur
she watches the monkeys
feeds them segments of orange
waits as the sun sets gold on the horizon
before venturing into the crowded streets

In a room in Rhodes she stares at the rosette
in the middle of the domed ceiling
for three days, too sick to move
On that island someone gave her a gift,
a small silver cornucopia which she wore
as a charm on a leather thong

Today the sadness envelopes her,
her loss, not a lover but a way of life,
like the shrivelled skins of old apples
which have lost their elasticity
her mood drops like lead

Gravity's rainbow could not fold
into the fall of her hair, nor its gold
be worth anything on the stock exchange

She winds her body in tissue and rolls
earthward like an Egyptian mummy
zigzagging, she reaches for the ground

She hears the cry of the muezzin
in the dusk of an Arabian sky,
sees the verticality of ziggurats,
the plasticity of domes,
smells the scent of the sacred rock

animal house

How long is a day?

They arrested us just before dawn.
Pulled from our narrow bed.
There was terror and a tearing
as if the body were separating from itself.

Would there be another day?

They took us to the animal house.
The stone-floored rooms
smelled of urine mixed with fear.

Time is filled with fear.

They put electrodes against my face,
against my neck,
against my tongue,
against my …

I recite the elements of my body.
Which body? My body? Your body?

The tongue swells in my mouth.
Will I ever feel again the nights of my tongue?

I am screaming from the inside,
I am screaming out loud

and there's no one who wants to listen
to the lesbian who's been tortured …

Can I live with the memory of this?

greek

for Suzanne Bellamy
in homage to Virginia Woolf, 1882-1941, who yearned to read Greek
and HD, 1886-1961, who learned to read Greek

She listened to the birds singing in Greek
but she could not understand them

this girl who would change the shape
of English literature

I want to learn Greek, she said to her tutor
You can't, he said, *for two reasons*

alpha: you're too young
beta: you're a girl

and so the birds sang on

o

Years later she returned to the song of birds
to their healing sounds

if only she could go some place quiet
be looked after, listen to the birds

understand their speech
unstop her ears

o

And so it was for that other
a poet who did read Greek

known only by her initials
for whom the world of Greece

was like Sophocles' birdsong
a poet visited and healed

as she lay in her bed with the waves
crashing at the foot of the Cornwell cliffs

o

Was it a lighthouse that brought her back?
Or was it the words she heard?

The hieroglyphs she saw? The sway of the boat
off the coast of Alexandria, at the port of Piraeus?

o

She said, *I defied them*
I have a friend, a poet

Who can read Greek
In secret I learned from her

It helped her unravel the birdsong
She heard them as they sang

witness to her Victorian violations
Their song the same as on the day

when Persephone was raped
and Zeus couldn't care less

o

On the days when she knew Greek
on these days she thought of Thoby

who was never too young
to learn Greek

on these days she understood
the bruising metaphors of Aeschylus

the tragedies of the Greek-speaking nightingale
of Antigone, the ecstacies of Agave

the songs of Sappho

o

There was a moment on a boat
when the light played just so

it was like that moment of understanding
the language of the birds

of what all that experience might mean
words   birdsong   Greek

oil and water

I said,
It's not rocket science to learn to care
for wildlife
for humanlife
for lesbianlife

I said,
There's a lesbian over there
in the souks and sands of Iraq
pulling in her headscarf
against desert storms

There's a lesbian over there
who in the dark of the moon
kisses the eyelids of her lover

There's a lesbian at risk
from bombs not of her own making

I said,
It'll be a moonless night
when the bombs begin to drop
silent as birdwing

She's about to be bombed alongside
the fathers
the brothers
the husbands she refused to marry

I said,
Long ago this land of Mesopotamia

running between the waters
of the Tigris and Euphrates
was a land friendly to women

No doubt the lesbian of that time
followed the path of the moon and
kissed the eyelids of her lover

I said,
She's about to be bombed
Because she doesn't care to leave
her home
her house
her lover

She's about to be bombed
for the viscous veins of oil
that lie beneath the ancient waters

They drained the marshes of
the Tigris and the Euphrates
to drill for oil

I said,
Have a look at the shape of
the fertile crescent

I said,
Like oil and water
lesbianlife and patriotism don't mix

the day of my crucifixion

for anyone who has experienced political betrayal

It was hot, an evening session of the court.
The prosecutor arrived with her senior counsel.

The committee aligned themselves.
The sycophants were there, their fig-filled pockets

ready to show the fruits of their plotting.
The victim sat surrounded by well-wishers.

The judge came in good time,
socialised with the prosecutor.

o

A few of my supporters arrived.

I sat as close as I could to those who
harboured ill will on their faces.

The judge explained the nature of the charge.
She outlined the protocol.

The victim chose to remain silent.
Her acolytes spoke for her.

I was permitted to speak only twice.
Once to correct the pronunciation of my name

(a simple enough affair)
and once to correct an error of history.

Halfway through the proceedings
they attached me to the bar with articulated weapons.

My shoulders ached in a memory of medieval justice.
My supporters attempted a futile protest.

Tears strolled down my face.
My movement restricted to a slight turn of the head.

After the testimonies they cut me down.

o

I walked out into the cooling moonrise air,
sat in silence and steeled myself to return.

Again I listened to fabricated, partial evidence.
There was no pity in that room.

Soon the court was over.
The kangaroo perched above the judge's head.

My head was uncovered.
We left, three of us, to debrief.

Two weeks later, sore from my injuries
I watched the main players

perform as if in a wake
ghostlike

They may have injured me,
but I remain.

I'm not dead yet.

song to purnululu

I was born on the ground
in the heat
and the dust

I was born on the ground
between the knees
of my mother
between the soaring
cliffs of my mother

I was born on the ground
between prickly spinifex
and shadeless mulga

I was born on the ground
and where I was born
the dust was as red
as my mother's blood
as red as my mother

I was born on the ground
and as I fell to the
red earth black cockatoos
flew overhead
screeching out their welcome

eye of a needle

Mid-twentieth century
They said I shouldn't live
You see, I'm a girl
My sister was not so lucky,
she died of preventable diarrhoea
My sisters are many
but the living not so numerous as the dead

o

I grow
I laugh
I learn to talk
Oh how I learn to talk
The school said there weren't enough desks
even for the boys
so I stayed home two more years

My mother told me stories
we picked herbs and fruits in the forest
we planted seeds
and we sang with the birds

o

At school no one noticed us much
until the day of the long black car
They took us to a place of
white floors

white people
white ceilings
I longed for
red earth
black people
blue skies

1970s
They cut the tongue
They break the words in my mouth
They make my body and my language homeless

o

The war comes
I escape
run the border
cross over
out of hell
into abandonment

I am nameless
my tongue straining for meaning
my language in exile

o

There is no one to love

o

1980s
In the camp I live under plastic
between lines of trauma
my lungs fill with mud
grief corrodes my heart

He stalks me
        hunts me like an animal
        takes me in a place
where only the birds can hear me scream

Day after day the birds wait
and listen for my cries

1990s
These are days of hope and despair
I am filling my mouth with new words
Words
        like "visa"
        like "protection"
        like "temporary"
Words shaped to fill other mouths

o

We women,
        our lives are like vines threading
The eye of a needle takes more than a camel

o

My daughter and I are growing together
We learn to read
        she almost a native speaker
        me with multiple vowels
        and crowding consonants
I practise when only the birds can hear me

o

Twenty-first century
There is no time for love
I learn the system
I know these walls
        for I have dug in the rubble
        and scaled them before

o

It is only then I find love
in unexpected places
She came into the centre
We were careful
It was slow but true
Daily we experiment with trust

o

Once long ago they said
I was a criminal
        for speaking my own language
Then I was a criminal
        because he raped me
They said I was a criminal
        because I fled their war into exile
In most parts of the world
        my love is criminal
And now that I am learning
        the methods
        and medicines
        of my foremothers
without a licence to practise my traditions
        I am a criminal

I do not need a licence to speak
I do not need a licence to love
I do not need a licence to heal
I do not need a licence to live

o

I still talk to the birds
I say, one day I will join you
One day it will be your turn
        to cry for me
On that day I want a sky burial

the name of god is o

The name of god is O
She was born in Baghdad
between the legs
of that fertile crescent

The O
The zero
invented here between the waters
of the Tigris and the Euphrates

The Gate of Ishtar shines
one hour's drive from Baghdad
Paradise, Eden's Garden,
the cradle ...
all rising out of the sand

Towers fall
like the speakers
incomprehensible
leaping from the listing Babel

The O
The zero
The zero and the one
are returning to Baghdad
in the shape of bombs

Babylon fell
Babylon with its

women falling, falling …
We are Babylonians

The one
Our godhead
the horror occurring
in the city
of too many nights

The one dropping
out of the sky
birds dying mid-flight
piercing the fragile O

Disney duplicates
replace the old languages
with the one true tongue
American English slipping
between the fissures

The centre of the world
It was here, they cry
now moved below the horizon
of the setting sun
Ishtar's sky boat
setting far too low

The zero and the one
the binary base prevailing
here in Baghdad

it was ancient time
it was Ur time

It was base ten
and base sixty
one to ten
one to sixty
one hour and one minute

The Hanging Gardens
wilt and die
The flowerbeds of
the Babylonians poisoned
by those proclaiming
one world
one market

How many bombs
can you drop
from an unpiloted aircraft
in one hour?
What is the power
of one?

How many years of history
can you decimate?
How many civilians
can you count
without the zero?

bibliography

Abbot, Sidney and Barbara Love. 1978. *Sappho was a Right-on Woman*. New York: Scarborough House.

Ascherson, Neal. 1996. *Black Sea: The Birthplace of Civilisation and Barbarism*. London: Vintage.

Albiston, Jordie. 1996. *Botany Bay Document: A Poetic History of the Women of Botany Bay*. Melbourne: Black Pepper Press.

Alexander, M. Jacqui. 2002. "Remembering *This Bridge*, Remembering Ourselves: Yearning, Memory and Desire." In Gloria Alexander and Analouise Keating (Eds.). *This Bridge We Call Home: Radical Visions for Transformation*. New York: Routledge.

Allen, Jeffner. 1986. *Lesbian Philosophy: Explorations*. Palo Alto, CA: Institute of Lesbian Studies.

—. 1991. "Passion in the Gardens of Delight". In Judith Barrington (Ed.). *An Intimate Wilderness*. Portland, OR: Eighth Mountain Press.

Allen, Paula Gunn. 1986. *The Sacred Hoop*. Boston: Beacon.

Amnesty International. 1997. *Breaking the Silence: Human rights violations based on sexual orientation*, London: Amnesty International United Kingdom.

—. 2001. *Crimes of hate, conspiracy of silence, Torture and ill-treatment based on sexual identity* ACT 40/016/2001.

Anzaldúa, Gloria. 1987. *Borderlands/La Frontera: The New Mestiza*. San Francisco: Spinsters/Aunt Lute.

Anzaldúa, Gloria E. and Analouise Keating (Eds.). 2002. *This Bridge We Call Home: Radical Visions for Transformation*. Routledge: New York.

Andrews, Munya. 2004. *The Seven Sisters of the Pleiades: Stories from around the World*. Melbourne: Spinifex Press.

Archer, Robyn. 1986. *Pack of Women*. Melbourne: Penguin Books.

Barnard, Mary. 1958. *Sappho: A New Translation*. Berkeley, Los Angeles and London: University of California Press.

Barnes, Djuna. 1936. *Nightwood*. London: Faber.

Baudelaire, Charles. 1857/1989. *The Flowers of Evil*. In Mathews, Marthiel and Jackson Mathews (Eds.). New York: New Directions.

Bellear, Lisa. 1996. "Chops 'n' Things" in *Dreaming in Urban Areas*. St Lucia: University of Queensland Press.

Biaggi, Cristina. 1994. *Habitations of the Great Goddess*. Manchester, CT: Knowledge, Ideas & Trends.

Bogin, Meg. 1976. *The Women Troubadors*. Scarborough, England: The Paddington Press.

Brooten, Bernadette J. 1996. *Love Between Women: Early Christian Responses to Female Homoeroticism*. Chicago: Chicago University Press.

Brossard, Nicole. 1998. *Mauve Desert*. Traslated by Susan de Lotbiniere-Harwood. Toronto: McCelland and Stewart.

Broumas, Olga. 1977. *Beginning with O.* New Haven and London: Yale University Press.

Broumas, Olga and T. Begley. 1994. *Sappho's Gymnasium*. Port Townsend: Copper Canyon Press.

Brown, Rita Mae. 1973. *Songs to a Handsome Woman*. Baltimore, MD: Diana Press.

—. 1974. *The Hand that Cradles the Rock*. Baltimore, MD: Diana Press.

Campbell, David A. 1982. *Greek Lyric Vol. 1*, Harvard University Press: Cambridge, MA.

Caputi, Jane. 2004. "Cuntspeak: Words from the heart of darkness." In Christine Stark and Rebecca Whisnant (Eds.). *Not For Sale: Feminists Resisting Prostitution and Pornography*. Melbourne: Spinifex Press. pp. 362-385.

Cohen, Dawn. 1989. "Lesbian Heaven". In Susan Hawthorne and Jenny Pausacker (Eds.). 1989. *Moments of Desire*. Melbourne: Penguin Books.

Covina, Gina and Laurel Galana (Eds.). 1975. *The Lesbian Reader*. Oakland, CA: Amazon Press.

Crow, Christine. 1990. *Miss X or the Wolf Woman*. London: The Women's Press.

Curb, Rosemary and Nancy Mannahan (Eds.). 1983. *Lesbian Nuns: Breaking the Silence* edited by Tallahassee, FL: Naiad.

Daly, Mary. 1978. *Gyn/Ecology: A Metaethics of Radical Feminism* Boston: Beacon Press.

Dauthendey, Elizabeth. 1906. *The Uranian Question and Women*. Leipzig.

DeJean, Joan. 1989. *Fictions of Sappho 1546-1937*. Chicago: University of Chicago Press.

de Pizan, Christine. 1982. *Book of the City of Ladies*. Translated by Earl Jeffrey Richards. Foreword by Marina Warner. New York: Persea Books

—. 1989. *Medieval Woman's Mirror of Honour*. Translated with an Introduction by Charity Cannon Willard. Edited with an Introduction by Madeleine Pelner Cosman. New York: Persea Books.

De Salvo, Louise and Mitchell A Leaska (Eds.). 1985. *The Letters of Vita Sackville-West to Virginia Woolf*. London: Macmillan.

de Veaux, Alexis. 2004. *Warrior Poet: A Biography of Audre Lorde*. New York: W.W. Norton.

Deming, Barbara. 1985. *A Humming Under My Feet: A Book of Travail*. London: The Women's Press.

Dickinson, Emily. 1960. *The Complete Poems of Emily Dickinson*. New York: Little Brown and Co.

Dobkin, Alix. 1999. "Lavender Jane is Born." *off our backs*, Vol. 29. No. 1. p. 12.

Doolittle, Hilda, (H.D.) 1972. *Hermetic Definition*. New York: New Directions.

—. 1973. *Trilogy*. New York: New Directions.

—. 1974. *Tribute to Freud*. Boston: David R. Godine.

—. 1981. *HERmione*. New York: New Directions.

—. 1983. *Collected Poems 1912-1944*. Edited by Louis L. Martz. New York: New Directions.

—. 1992. *Paint It Today*. Edited and with an Introduction by Cassandra Laity. New York: New York University Press.

DuBois, Page. 1995. *Sappho is Burning*. London and Chicago: University of Chicago Press.

DuPlessis, Rachel Blau. 1986. *H.D.: The Career of That Struggle*. Brighton, Sussex: Harvester.

Dunsford, Cathie. 1997. *The Journey Home / Te Haerenga Kainga*. Melbourne: Spinifex Press.

—. 2001. *Song of the Selkies*. Melbourne: Spinifex Press.

Dunsford, Cathie and Susan Hawthorne (Eds.). 1990. *The Exploding Frangipani*. Auckland: New Women's Press.

Dworkin, Andrea. 1980. "The simple story of a lesbian girlhood". *The New Woman's Broken Heart*. East Palo Alto, CA: Frog In the Well.

Dykewomon, Elana. 2003. *Beyond the Pale*. Vancouver, BC: Raincoast Books.

Eldershaw, M. Barnard. 1966. *A House is Built*. Sydney and London: Australasian Publishing Company in Association with George G. Harrap and Co. Ltd.

Elgin, Suzette Haden. 2000. *Native Tongue*. New York: The Feminist Press; Melbourne: Spinifex Press.

Faderman, Lillian. 1981. *Surpassing the Love of Men*. New York: William Morrow and Company.

Fairbairns, Zoë. 1988. "Interview with Marjorie Barnard" in *Writing Lives: Conversations between Women Writers*, edited by Mary Chamberlain. London: Virago.

Falk, Barbara. With Cecile Trioli. 2000. *D.J. Dorothy Jean Ross 1891-1982*. Melbourne: Melbourne University Press.

Feinberg, Lesley. 1993. *Stone Butch Blues*. Ithaca, NY: Firebrand Books.

Fergus, Lara. 2005. "Lifeboat". In "Elsewhere in Every Country: Locating Lesbian Writing." Performed at the 3rd Feminist Studies in Literature Conference, Seoul, Korea. 21 June 2005.

Fischer, Erica. 1996. *Aimée and Jaguar*. Translated by Edna McCown. London: Bloomsbury.

Fisher, John. 1986, *The Companion to Roses*. Harmondsworth: Penguin.

Fleming, Lee. 1995. *To Sappho, My Sister: Lesbian Sisters Write About Their Lives*. Charlottetown, PEI: Gynergy; Melbourne: Spinifex Press.

Fletcher, Beryl. 2002. *The Word Burners*. Melbourne: Spinifex Press.

Fletcher, Lynne Yamaguchi and Adrien Saks (Eds.). 1990. *Lavender Lists*. Boston, MA: Alyson Publications.

Fonseca, Lariane. 1992. *If Passion Were a Flower...* Melbourne: Spinifex Press.

Frankfort-Nachmias, Chava and Erella Shadmi (Eds.). 2005. *Sappho in the Holy Land: Lesbian Existence and Dilemmas in Contemporary Israel*. Albany, NY: State University of New York Press.

Friedman, Susan Stanford. 1990. *Persephone's Web: Gender, Modernity, H.D.'s Fiction*. Cambridge: Cambridge University Press.

Gage, Carolyn. 2004. *off our backs*, Vol. 33, Nos. 5/6, pp. 56-7. p. 12 and p. 13.

Gardner, Kay. 1997. *Sounding the Inner Landscape*. Rockport, MA and Brisbane: Element Books.

Gearheart, Sally. 1979. *The Wanderground: Stories of the Hill Women*. Watertown, MA: Persephone Press.

Gimbutas, Marija. 1990. *The Language of the Goddess*. San Francisco: Harper and Row. London: Thames and Hudson.

—. 1990. Lecture, UCLA, May 5.

Glamuzina, Julie and Alison J. Laurie. 1991. *Parker and Hulme* Auckland: New Women's Press.

Grahn, Judy. 1978. *The Work of a Common Woman*. Baltimore, MD: Diana Press.

—. 1982. *The Queen of Wands*. Trumansburg, NY: The Crossing Press.

—. 1984. *Another Mother Tongue: Gay Words, Gay Worlds.* Boston: Beacon Press.

—. 1985. *The Highest Apple: Sappho and the Lesbian Poetic Tradition.* San Francisco: Spinsters/Aunt Lute.

—. 1987. *The Queen of Swords*. Boston: Beacon Press.

Guerrilla Girls. 1998. *The Guerrilla Girls' Bedside Companion to the History of Western Art.* New York: Penguin Books.

Hampton, Susan. 1989. *Surly Girls*. Sydney: Collins.

Hanscombe, Gillian. 1992. *Sybil: The Glide of Her Tongue.* Melbourne: Spinifex Press.

—. 1995. *Figments of a Murder*. Melbourne: Spinifex Press.

Hanscombe, Gillian and Virgina P.M. Smyers. 1987. *Writing for their Lives: The Modernist Women, 1900-1940.* London: The Women's Press.

Hardy, Sara. 2005. *The Unusual Life of Edna Walling*. Sydney: Allen and Unwin.

Harrison, Jane Ellen. 1903. *Prolegomena to the Study of Greek Religion.* Cambridge: Cambridge University Press.

—. 1912. *Themis: A Study of the Social Origins of Greek Religion.* Cambridge: Cambridge University Press.

Harron, Mary and Daniel Minahan. 1995. *I Shot Andy Warhol*. New York: Grove Press.

Hart, Ellen Louise and Martha Nell Smith (Eds.). 1998. *Open Me Carefully: Emily Dickinson's Intimate Letters to Susan Huntington Dickinson*. Ashfield, MA: Paris Press.

Hawthorne, Susan. 1982. *The Homeric Hymns to Demeter and Aphrodite*. Unpublished.

—. 1992. *The Falling Woman*. Melbourne: Spinifex Press (reprinted 2003).

—. 1989. "Erotica Alphabetica." In Susan Hawthorne and Jenny Pausacker (Eds.). *Moments of Desire*. Melbourne: Penguin Books.

—. 1993. "Diotima Speaks through the Body". In *Engendering Origins: Critical Feminist Essays in Plato and Aristotle*, Bat-Ami Bar On (Ed.). State University of New York Press, Albany.
—. 1997. "Dialogues with Love". In *Fruit Salad*. Sydney: Sydney Gay and Lesbian Mardi Gras.
—. 1999. "Seized: Variations on Sappho's Fragment 31". In Susan Hawthorne. *Bird*. Melbourne: Spinifex Press.
—. 2003. "The Depoliticising of Lesbian Culture." *Hecate*, Vol. 29, No. 2, pp. 235-247.
—. 2004a. "Research and Silence: Why the torture of lesbians is invisible." Women's Studies Association (NZ), Collected Papers and Presentations. Wellington: WSA (NZ). pp. 64-72.
—. 2004b. "A Family Fable." *Hecate,* Vol. 30, No. 2, pp. 127-128; *Rain and Thunder* (USA) No. 25, Winter, p. 33.
Hawthorne, Susan, Cathie Dunsford and Susan Sayer (Eds.). 1997. *Car Maintenance, Explosives and Love and Other Contemporary Lesbian Writings*. Melbourne: Spinifex Press.
Hennegan, Alison (Ed.). 2000. *The Lesbian Pillow Book.* London: Fourth Estate.
Hobby, Elaine and Chris White (Eds.). 1991. *What Lesbians Do in Books*. London: The Women's Press.
Hope, Emily. 1983. *The Legend of Pope Joan*. Melbourne: Sisters Publishing.
Hossain, Rokeya Sakhawat. 1988. *Sultana's Dream and Selections from The Secluded Ones*. New York: The Feminist Press.
Howe, Susan. 1993 *The Birthmark: Unsettling the Wilderness in American Literary History*. Middletown, CT: Wesleyan University Press.

Irwin, Sally. 2000. *Between Heaven and Earth: The Life of Mountaineer, Freda du Faur.* Melbourne: White Crane Press.
Ishida, Tomiye. "Tsuki ga Deta". In C. Allyson Lee and Makeda Silvera (Eds.). 1995. *Pearls of Passion*. Toronto: Sister Vision Press.
Izumo, Marou and Clare Maree. 2000. *Love upon the Chopping Board*. Melbourne: Spinifex Press.

Jackson, Donna. 1997. "Car Maintenance, Explosives and Love". In Susan Hawthorne, Cathie Dunsford and Susan Sayer (Eds.). *Car Maintencance, Explosives and Love and Other Contemporary Lesbian Writings*. Melbourne: Spinifex Press.

Jay, Karla. 1999. *Tales of the Lavender Menace: A Memoir of Liberation*. New York: Basic Books.

Jeffs, Sandy. *Poems from the Madhouse*. 2000. Melbourne: Spinifex Press.

Jekyll, Gertrude. 1902/1983. *Roses for English Gardens*. London: Penguin Books, co-authored with Edward Mawley, Revised by Graham Stuart Thomas.

Johnson, Eva. 1990. "Alison". In Cathie Dunsford and Susan Hawthorne (Eds.). *The Exploding Frangipani*. Auckland: New Women's Press.

— "What Do They Call Me?". In Dale Spender (Ed.). *Heroines*. Melbourne: Penguin; Bruce Parr. (Ed.). 1996. *Australian Gay and Lesbian Plays*. Sydney: Currency Press.

Kelly, Jennifer. 2005. *Zest for Life: Lesbians' Experiences of Menopause*. Melbourne: Spinifex Press.

Labarge, Margaret Wade. 1987. *Women in Medieval Life*. London: Hamish Hamilton.

Langley, Eve. 1942/2002. *The Pea Pickers*. Sydney: Angus and Robertson.

Liddell and Scott. 1986. *Greek-English Lexicon*. Oxford University Press.

Liddington, Jill. 1998. *Female Fortune: Land Gender and Authority, The Anne Lister Diaries and Other Writings, 1833-36*. London: Rivers Oram Press.

Lorde, Audre. 1982. *Zami: An Autobiographical Myth*. Trumansburg, NY: The Crossing Press.

Lugones, Maria. 2003. *Pilgrimages/Peregrinajes: Theorizing Coalition against Multiple Oppressions*. Lanham: Rowman and Littlefield.

Mackay, Anne (Ed.). 1993. *Wolf Girls at Vassar*. New York: St Martin's Press.

Mackinnon, Ian. 1998. "Film's followers fight fire with fire." *The Australian*. 9 December. p. 9.

Manji, Irshad. 2003. *The Trouble with Islam: A Muslim's Call for Reform of Her Faith*. Sydney: Random House.

Marchessault, Jovette. 1985. *Lesbian Triptych*. Translated by Yvonne M. Klein. Toronto: Women's Press.

Marsh, Jan. 1994. *Christina Rosetti: A Literary Biography*. London: Pimlico.

Mavor, Elizabeth. 1973. *The Ladies of Llangollen: A Study of Romantic Friendship*. London: Penguin.

McKinley, Catherine E. and Joyce DeLaney (Eds.). 1995. *Afrekete: An Anthology of Black Lesbian Writing*. New York: Anchor Books.

McSkimming, Donna. 1986. *Beware the Bougainvillea*. Adelaide: Friendly Street Poets. pp. 8-9.

—. 1992. "Ocean Travelling". In *Three's Company. Poems by Deborah McCulloch, Donna McSkimming, Elizabeth Biff Ward*. Adelaide: Friendly Street Poets

Meigs, Mary. 1981. *Lily Briscoe: A Self Portrait* Vancouver: Talonbooks.

Min, Anchee. 1994. *Red Azalea*. London: Victor Gollancz.

Miner, Valerie. 1982. *Blood Sisters*. New York: St Martin's Press.

Mitchell, Juliet and Jacqueline Rose (Eds.). 1982. *Feminine Sexuality: Jacques Lacan and the École Freudienne*. Macmillan, London.

Morgan, Elaine. 1973. *The Descent of Woman*. New York: Bantam.

Morgan, Robin. ND. *Monster*. Melbourne: Radical Feminists.

—. 1992. "The Word of a Woman" in *The Word of a Woman: Selected Prose 1968-1992*. New York: W.W. Norton; London: Virago.

Moorhead, Finola. 1987. *Remember the Tarantella*. 1987. Sydney: Primavera Press; London: The Women's Press

—. 2000. *Darkness More Visible*. Melbourne: Spinifex Press.

Moss, Merrilee. 2001. *Fedora Walks*. Melbourne: Spinifex Press

Namjoshi, Suniti. 1985. *The Conversations of Cow*. London: The Women's Press.

—. 1993. *St Suniti and the Dragon*. Melbourne: Spinifex Press.

—. 1996. *Building Babel*. Melbourne: Spinifex Press; London: Virago.

—. 2000. *Goja: An Autobiographical Myth*. Melbourne: Spinifex Press.

Namjoshi, Suniti and Gillian Hanscombe. 1986. *Flesh and Paper*. Seaton, England: Jezebel Tapes and Books.

Niederer, Barbara. 1995. "Women in Chinese Script". In C*hina for Women: Travel and Culture*. New York: The Feminist Press; Melbourne: Spinifex Press.

Nwapa, Flora. 1986. *Cassava Song and Rice Song*. Lagos: Tana Press.

Peacock, Sandra J. 1988. *Jane Ellen Harrison: The Mask and the Self*. London and New Haven: Yale University Press

Porter, Dorothy. 1996. *Crete*. Melbourne: Hyland House.

Post, Sue-Ann. 2005. *The Confessions of an Unrepentant Lesbian Ex-Mormon*. Sydney: ABC Books

Radicalesbians. 1970. "The Woman-Identified-Woman". In Rosemary Silva (Ed.). *Lesbian Quotations*. Boston, MA: Alyson Publications.

Raymond, Janice. 1986. *A Passion for Friends: Toward a Philosophy of Female Affection*. Boston: Beacon Press; London: The Women's Press, 1989. Reprinted 2001. Melbourne: Spinifex Press.

Reinfelder, Moniker. 1996. "Persecution and Resistance". In Monika Reinfelder (Ed.). *Amazon to Zami: Toward a global lesbian feminism*. London: Cassell.

Rexroth, Kenneth and Ling Chung (Eds. and Trans.). 1982. *Women Poets of China*. New York: New Directions Press.

Reynolds, Margaret (Ed.). 1993. *Penguin Anthology of Lesbian Short Stories*. London: Penguin Books.

Rich, Adrienne. 1973. *Diving into the Wreck*. New York: W.W. Norton and Company.

—. 1978. "Twenty-One Love Poems". In *The Dream of a Common Language: Poems 1974-1977*. New York: W.W. Norton and Company.

Rivera-Fuentes, Consuelo and Lynda Birke. 2001. "Talking With/In Pain: Reflections on bodies under torture". *Women's Studies International Forum 24*, (6): 653-668.

Robinson, Portia. 1988. *The Women of Botany Bay: A Reinterpretation of the Role of Women in the Origins of Australian Society*. Sydney: The Macquarie Library.

Rosetti, Christina. 1994. *Goblin Market and other poems*. Mineola, New York: Dover Publications.

Roy, Arundhati. 2004. "Do Turkeys Enjoy Thanksgiving." World Social Forum, Mumbai. 16 January.

Rushby, Kevin. 2003. *Children of Kali*. Delhi: Penguin Books.

Sackville-West, Vita. 1987. *The Illustrated Garden Book*. London: Michael Joseph.

—. 1989. *The Land and The Garden*. Exeter, Devon: Webb and Bower.

Sapphire. 1997. *Push*. New York: Vintage.

"Sappho Lost Poem Found". 2005. *Weekend Australian*, 2-3 July, p. 25.

Schoppmann, Claudia. 1996. *Days of Masquerade: Life stories of lesbians during the Third Reich*. Translated by Allison Brown. New York: Columbia University Press,

Secrest, Meryle. 1976. *Between Me and Life: A biography of Romaine Brooks*. London: Macdonald and Jane's.

Sei Shonagon. 1928. *The Pillow Book of Sei Shonagon.* Translated by Arthur Waley. London: George Allen and Unwin.

Shaktini, Namascar. 1982. "Displacing the Phallic Subject". *Signs*, Vol. 8, No. 1. pp. 29-44.

—. (Ed.). 2005. *On Monique Witting: Theoretical, Political, and Literary Essays*. Urbana and Chicago: University of Illinois Press.

Silko, Leslie Marmon. 1991. *Almanac of the Dead*. New York: Penguin.

Smedley, Agnes. 1995. "Silk Workers". In *China for Women: Travel and Culture*. Melbourne: Spinifex Press; New York: The Feminist Press. pp. 47-52.

Smith, Jenn. 2000. "Tsitsi Tiripano: Fighting for Lesbian and Gay Rights in Zimbabwe." *off our backs*, Vol. 30, No. 4. pp. 1 and 6-7.

Snyder, Jane McIntosh. 1997. *Lesbian Desire in the Lyrics of Sappho*, New York: Columbia University Press.

Solanas, Valerie. 1967. *SCUM Manifesto*. New York: The Olympia Press.

Spender, Dale (Ed.). 1991. *Heroines: A Contemporary Anthology of Australian Women Writers*. Melbourne: Penguin Books.

Stein, Gertrude. 1935. *Lectures in America*. New York: Random House.

—. 1971. *Look at Me Now and Here I Am: Writings and Lectures, 1909-45*, Patricia Meyerowitz (Ed.). Harmondsworth: Penguin Books.

—. 1988. *The World is Round*. San Francisco: North Point Press.

—. 1989. *Lifting Belly*. Rebecca Mark (Ed.). Tallahassee, FL: Naiad.

Sukthankar, Ashwini (Ed.). 1999. *Facing the Mirror: Lesbian Writing from India*. Delhi: Penguin Books.

Taylor, Jean. 2000. *The C-Word*. Melbourne: Spinifex Press.

Taylor, Margaret. 1989. "World's Oldest Lesbian Dies: Monte Punshon 1882-1989." *Melbourne Star Observer*. p. 1 and p. 3.

Teish, Luisah. 1988. *Jumbalayah: The Natural Woman's Book of Personal and Practical Rituals*: San Francisco: HarperSan Francisco.

Thadani, Giti. 1996. *Sakhiyani: Lesbian Desire in Ancient and Modern India*. London and New York: Cassell.

—. 2004. *Moebius Trip*. Melbourne: Spinifex; Delhi: Penguin Books.

The Art of Lesbian Love. London: Hamlyn.

Torton Beck, Evelyn (Ed.). 1982. *Nice Jewish Girls: A Lesbian Anthology*. Watertown, MA: Persephone Press.

Tsukiyama, Gail. 1993. *Women of the Silk*. New York: St Martin's Press.

Turner, Kay. 1996. *Dear Sappho: A Legacy of Lesbian Love Letters*. London: Thames and Hudson.

Undset, Sigrid. 1951/1980. *Kristin Lavransdatter*. London: Picador.

Vivien, Renée. 1983. *The Woman of the Wolf and other stories*. Translated by Karla Jay and Yvonne M. Klein. New York: Gay Presses of New York.

VS. 1999. "How Does it Feel to be a 'Problem'?" In Ashwini Sukthankar (Ed.). *Facing the Mirror: Lesbian Writing from India*. Delhi: Penguin.

Walker, Barbara. 1983. *The Woman's Encyclopedia of Myths and Secrets*. San Francisco: HarperSanFrancisco..

Weigle, Marta. 1982. *Spiders and Spinsters: Women and Mythology*. Albuquerque: University of New Mexico Press.

Welch, Liz. 2000. "Tsitsi Tiripano: Matters of the heart politicise an accidental activist." *Ms Magazine*, June/July. pp 12-15.

Williamson, Margaret. 1995. *Sappho's Immortal Daughters*. Cambridge, MA and London: Harvard University Press.

Winterson, Jeanette. 1987. *The Passion*. London: Bloomsbury.

—. 1989. *Sexing the Cherry*. London: Bloomsbury.

—. 1993. *Written on the Body*. London: Vintage.

—. 2005. *Lighhousekeeping*. London: Perennial.

Wittig, Monique. 1972. *Les Guérillères*. London: Picador.

—. 1975. *The Lesbian Body*, London: Peter Owen.

—. 1987. *Across the Acheron*. London: Peter Owen.

—. 1992. *The Straight Mind and Other Essays*. Boston: Beacon Press.

Wittig, Monique and Sande Zeig. 1979. *Lesbian Peoples*. New York: Avon Books.

Woolf, Virginia. 1990. *To the Lighthouse*, London: The Hogarth Press.

—. 1929/2002. *A Room of One's Own*. London: Penguin.

—. 1968. "On not knowing Greek". In *The Common Reader: First series*. London: The Hogarth Press.

—. 1969. *The Waves*. Harmondsworth: Penguin.

Yates, Frances. 1978. *The Art of Memory*. Harmondsworth: Penguin Books.

Zimmerman, Bonnie. 1990. *The Safe Sea of Women: Lesbian Fiction 1969-1989*. Boston: Beacon Press.

films

Barrett, Shirley. 1996. *Love Serenade*. Jan Chapman Productions. Aust.
Brooks, Sue. 1997. *The Road to Nhill*. Gecko Films. Aust.
—. 2004. *Japanese Story*. Gecko Films. Aust.
Courtin-Wilson, Amiel. 2000. *Chasing Buddha*. Halo Films. Aust.
Gorriss, Marleen. 1981. *A Question of Silence*. Netherlands. *De Stilte and Christine M* (The Silence Around Christine M).
Hammer, Barbara. 1995. *Tender Fictions*. Barbara Hammer Films. USA.
Harron, Mary. 1996. *I Shot Andy Warhol*. Taylor Made. USA/GB.
Jackson, Peter. 1994. *Heavenly Creatures*. Miramax. NZ/France/Ger.
Mehta, Deepa. 1996. *Fire*. Trial by Fire. Can.

acknowledgements

Some of the poems in this collection have been previously published, occasionally in very different forms. I'd like to thank the following journals, online literary media, newspapers and radio for their support: *Divan* (online), *Heat*, *OzPoet* (online), *Lesbiana*, *Overland*, *Common…Places* (online), *Suniti Namjoshi Homepage* (online), *Absolutely Women's Health*, *Experimedia* (online), *Hecate*, *Thylazine* (online), *The Box Seat*, ABC Radio National, and especially Barry Hill of *The Australian*. Others have appeared in anthologies and I thank the editors of *Interior Despots: Running the Border* edited by Sue Moss and Karen Knight; Pardalote Press, 2001; *Car Maintenance, Explosives and Love and Other Lesbian Writings* edited by Cathie Dunsford, Susan Hawthorne and Susan Sayer, Spinifex Press, 1997; *Body Lines*, edited by Jillian Bartlett and Cathi Joseph. Redress Women's Press, 1991; *Breaking Free* edited by Beatriz Copello and Robyn Lanssen, Bemac Publications, 2004.

Two poems were performed by the Performing Older Women's Circus as physical theatre pieces: *Unstopped Mouths*, The Pit Theatre, Footscray Community Arts Centre, 1997; *Carnivale*, Swinburne University, Lilydale Campus, 1998. Some sections of Rose Garden were incorporated into the script of *The Maiden Aunt's Story*, Gay Games, Paddington Town Hall, Sydney, 2002. Three poems have been performed as solo or duo performances: *Gravity Defied*. 3rd Melbourne Poetry Festival Opening Night. Chapel Off Chapel, Melbourne, 2001; Townsville International Women's Conference, 2002; Byron Bay Writers' Festival, 2002; Gay Games, Newtown New Works, New Theatre, King Street, Newtown, Sydney, 2002; *Animal House*, Massey University Events Centre, Palmerston North, New Zealand, 2003; *Greek. Doors, Rooms … and Going Up the Wall*, performance with Gayle McPherson in conjunction with exhibition of art works by Suzanne Bellamy, 2004. *Eye of a needle* was commissioned by the 10th International Women's Health Meeting, New Delhi, India 2005.

The series of poems entitled "Unstopped Mouths" was written with the assistance of a Developing Writers' Grant from Arts Victoria, 1998.

If I were to acknowledge all the works that have gone into this collection of poems the list of sources would be longer than the poems themselves. Sometimes I have used a word, a small phrase, a concept. Sometimes a poem, a work of art, a woman's life, an experience, or a passing comment has provided the core of a line or a poem. I have acknowledged these throughout the poems.

There are also women who have continued to nurture me. Their contribution cannot be measured. I cannot weight the ways in which they have changed my life. They have sometimes made it bearable; at other times they have brought me enormous joy; they have challenged me with honesty; and they have been interested. I cannot name all whose lives have moved me, but I will name those who've had a direct impact on this book. I would like to thank the women at Spinifex Press: Maralann Damiano for keeping me sane (and tidy); Belinda Morris for her editorial eagle eye; Jo O'Brien for her financial discernment; and Deb Snibson for the design and typesetting of this book. I have been lucky to have editorial feedback from four poets. I would like to thank Suniti Namjoshi for her generous editing of my work, especially "India Sutra". Judith Rodriguez responded with in-depth comments on "Unstopped Mouths" including its layout, while Lizz Murphy gave me early feedback on this series. Patricia Sykes read early drafts of "Unstopped Mouths" and gave all of *The Butterfly Effect* her precise attention at a very late stage, and I am indebted to her for her challenges and detailed comments. I thank them all for their poetic acumen and for saving me from syntactic and semantic embarrassment (any errors are my oversight). Thanks to: Donna Jackson and Jean Taylor who enticed me into circus and into its many pathways through fear and performance; Suzanne Bellamy for art and life; Diane Bell for friendship and a reference; Meryl Waugh for her stargazing and farsightedness; Coleen Clare for her strength and honesty; Zohl dé Ishtar for camp fire stories; Lariane Fonseca for travels in India and a lesbian visual aesthetic; Kaye Moseley for a quarter of a century of conversations and coffee; my dog River for her patience and joyousness; and to my partner, Renate Klein for her great spirit of generosity, her passionate engagement with life, and her love.